CRACK THE DATA ANALYST INTERVIEW

REAL-TIME QUESTIONS & EXPERT ANSWERS

YASH D.

CRACK THE DATA ANALYST INTERVIEW: REAL-TIME QUESTIONS & EXPERT ANSWERS
First edition. February 28, 2025.

Written by Yash d.

Table of Contents

To all the aspiring data analysts who are tirelessly preparing, refining their skills, and chasing their dream roles—this book is for you.

To those burning the midnight oil, running SQL queries one last time, debugging Python scripts, and revisiting probability concepts before the big day—your hard work will pay off.

To everyone who has faced rejection but refused to give up, who believes in the power of data to drive decisions, and who knows that every challenge is just another problem waiting to be solved—keep pushing forward.

This book is dedicated to your journey, your perseverance, and your success. May it be the guide that helps you crack your next interview and land the role you deserve.

Preface

In today's data-driven world, the demand for skilled data analysts has never been higher. Organizations across industries—whether tech giants, financial institutions, healthcare companies, or e-commerce platforms—are leveraging data to make informed decisions, optimize processes, and enhance customer experiences. As a result, companies are on the lookout for data professionals who can extract insights from data, communicate findings effectively, and drive strategic business outcomes.

If you're reading this book, chances are you're preparing for a data analyst interview. You might be transitioning into the field from another domain, stepping into the workforce for the first time, or looking to advance your career by securing a coveted role at a top company. Regardless of where you are in your journey, **"Crack the Data Analyst Interview: Real-Time Questions & Expert Answers"** is designed to be your ultimate guide to acing the interview process and landing the job you deserve.

Why This Book?

INTERVIEW PREPARATION can feel overwhelming. There is a vast amount of knowledge to cover—SQL, statistics, Python, business analytics, data visualization, case studies, and behavioral questions. Many candidates struggle with structuring their study plan, identifying key concepts to focus on, and understanding what interviewers truly expect.

This book takes the guesswork out of interview preparation by providing a **structured, practical, and targeted** approach to mastering data analyst interviews. It is designed to help you:

- **Understand Real-World Interview Scenarios:** We have compiled **real-time questions** asked by top companies, ensuring that you are practicing with actual interview material rather than generic theory.

- **Gain Concise and Expert Answers:** Instead of vague explanations, we provide clear, precise, and structured answers that mirror how an experienced analyst would respond in an interview.

- **Master Technical and Business Questions:** This book covers **SQL, Python, statistics, probability, A/B testing, business analytics, and case studies**, ensuring you are well-prepared for both technical and non-technical discussions.

- **Develop Critical Thinking for Case Studies:** FAANG and other leading companies often test problem-solving abilities through case studies. We provide frameworks to **structure your thought process**, analyze data effectively, and present compelling recommendations.

- **Refine Your Communication and Behavioral Skills:** Landing a job is not just about technical expertise; interviewers evaluate how well you communicate your findings, handle pressure, and work with cross-functional teams. This book equips you with **behavioral question strategies** using the STAR framework.

What to Expect from This Book?

THIS BOOK IS DIVIDED into multiple sections to streamline your preparation and maximize efficiency.

1. Understanding the Data Analyst Role

BEFORE JUMPING INTO technical questions, it is crucial to understand the core responsibilities of a data analyst, the tools commonly used, and how companies evaluate candidates. This section helps you:

- Get familiar with different types of data analyst roles (e.g., product, marketing, finance)

- Understand key skills and tools required (SQL, Python, Excel, Tableau, Power BI)

- Learn what hiring managers look for in candidates

2. Technical Interview Preparation

THE BACKBONE OF ANY data analyst interview is **technical proficiency**. In this section, we break down the most frequently tested topics:

- **SQL Mastery:** Writing complex queries, optimizing performance, handling missing data, working with joins, window functions, and CTEs.

- **Python and Pandas:** Data manipulation, working with large datasets, handling missing values, and visualizing data.

- **Statistics & Probability:** Hypothesis testing, confidence intervals, probability distributions, and A/B testing.

Each question is paired with a well-structured answer and real-world application, so you don't just memorize concepts—you **understand how to apply them in business scenarios**.

3. Business & Product Analytics

DATA ANALYSTS MUST bridge the gap between data and business decisions. This section teaches you how to:

- **Analyze key business metrics** like customer churn, lifetime value (CLV), and conversion rates

- **Evaluate A/B test results** and determine statistical significance

- **Interpret data trends and provide actionable recommendations**

4. Case Study Approach for FAANG Interviews

TOP TECH COMPANIES test candidates through open-ended case studies where you must think on your feet. This section equips you with:

- A structured approach to **solving ambiguous business problems**
- Frameworks like **SPADE (Situation, Problem, Analysis, Data, Execution)**
- Sample case studies with detailed answers to simulate real interview scenarios

5. Behavioral & Communication Skills

A STRONG TECHNICAL skillset alone is not enough. Interviewers assess your problem-solving approach, teamwork, and ability to communicate insights effectively. This section helps you:

- Answer **behavioral questions using the STAR (Situation, Task, Action, Result) method**
- Present data findings in a clear, concise, and compelling manner
- Handle tricky interview situations, such as answering questions when you don't know the exact solution

6. Last-Minute Revision Strategies

THE FINAL DAYS BEFORE your interview are crucial. This section provides:

- A **checklist of must-know concepts**
- Quick summaries of key formulas and SQL functions
- Time management tips to stay focused and confident

How to Use This Book Effectively?

TO GET THE MOST OUT of this book, follow these best practices:

1. **Start with a Self-Assessment:** Identify your strengths and weaknesses in SQL, Python, statistics, and business analytics. This will help you focus on areas that need improvement.
2. **Follow a Structured Study Plan:** Spend time on each section based on your needs. If SQL is your weak point, allocate extra hours to practicing queries.
3. **Practice Hands-On:** Don't just read SQL queries or Python scripts—**write them in a coding environment**. Use real datasets to solidify your understanding.
4. **Simulate Real Interview Conditions:** Time yourself while answering questions, especially case studies. **Practice explaining your thought process aloud**, as you would in an actual interview.
5. **Refine Your Communication Skills:** Clear and concise explanations are just as important as getting the right answer. Focus on **storytelling with data**—how you present insights matters.
6. **Review and Iterate:** Keep track of mistakes and revisit tough concepts. Consistent revision is key to retention.

Who Should Read This Book?

THIS BOOK IS TAILORED for:

- **Aspiring Data Analysts** looking for their first job or internship
- **Professionals transitioning into data analytics** from another field
- **Experienced analysts preparing for FAANG and top tech interviews**
- **Students and recent graduates** who want to build a strong technical foundation

Whether you're preparing for an entry-level analyst role or aiming for a senior position, the insights and strategies in this book will help you approach your interview with confidence and clarity.

Final Thoughts

ACING A DATA ANALYST interview is not just about memorizing technical concepts—it's about **understanding how to apply your skills to real-world business problems**. This book is meant to be more than just an interview guide; it is a roadmap to help you become a well-rounded data professional.

Remember, every interview is an opportunity to **learn, improve, and grow**. Even if you face rejection, treat it as a stepping stone toward success. Each setback refines your approach, and with persistence, you will land the role that's right for you.

Data is shaping the future, and as a data analyst, you are at the forefront of this transformation. Your ability to derive insights from raw numbers, tell stories with data, and drive meaningful decisions makes you a valuable asset to any organization.

So, stay curious, keep practicing, and trust the process. You are closer to your dream job than you think.

Let's get started—your journey to cracking the data analyst interview begins now.

Chapter 1: Understanding the Data Analyst Role

Key Responsibilities and Expectations

1. What are the primary responsibilities of a data analyst?

A data analyst plays a crucial role in gathering, processing, and analyzing data to help businesses make informed decisions. The primary responsibilities include:

- **Data Collection & Extraction:** Gathering raw data from databases, APIs, spreadsheets, and other sources.
- **Data Cleaning & Processing:** Identifying missing values, handling inconsistencies, and transforming data for better analysis.
- **Data Analysis & Interpretation:** Using statistical methods and tools to uncover trends, patterns, and correlations.
- **Data Visualization:** Creating dashboards, charts, and reports to present findings in an understandable way.
- **Stakeholder Communication:** Collaborating with teams to translate data insights into business actions.
- **Performance Monitoring:** Tracking key performance indicators (KPIs) and suggesting improvements.

- **Process Automation:** Writing scripts or using tools to automate repetitive data tasks.

2. How does a data analyst differ from a data scientist?

WHILE BOTH ROLES DEAL with data, their focus areas are different:

- **Data Analyst:** Primarily works with structured data, using SQL, Excel, and visualization tools to interpret past and present trends.

- **Data Scientist:** Focuses more on predictive modeling, machine learning, and advanced statistical techniques using programming languages like Python and R.

3. What tools do data analysts commonly use?

DATA ANALYSTS RELY on a variety of tools, including:

- **SQL:** For querying and manipulating databases.

- **Excel:** For data organization, pivot tables, and basic statistical analysis.

- **Tableau/Power BI:** For creating interactive dashboards.

- **Python/R:** For advanced analysis and automation.

- **Google Analytics:** For web data analysis.

- **ETL Tools:** Such as Alteryx, Apache NiFi, and Talend for data transformation.

4. Can you explain the data analysis process?

THE DATA ANALYSIS PROCESS involves the following steps:

1. **Defining the Problem:** Understanding business objectives and key questions.
2. **Collecting Data:** Extracting data from relevant sources.

3. **Cleaning and Preparing Data:** Handling missing values, removing duplicates, and ensuring accuracy.
4. **Exploring Data:** Conducting initial exploratory data analysis (EDA) to identify patterns.
5. **Performing Analysis:** Using statistical techniques, regression models, and visualization.
6. **Interpreting and Presenting Findings:** Communicating insights through reports and dashboards.
7. **Making Data-Driven Decisions:** Providing recommendations based on insights.

5. What are some key SQL functions every data analyst should know?

SOME ESSENTIAL SQL functions include:

- SELECT: Retrieve specific data from a table.
- JOIN: Combine data from multiple tables.
- GROUP BY: Aggregate data based on specific attributes.
- HAVING: Filter aggregated results.
- CASE: Implement conditional logic.
- WINDOW FUNCTIONS: Perform advanced aggregations like running totals and rank calculations.

6. How do you ensure data accuracy in your analysis?

ENSURING DATA ACCURACY is critical, and can be achieved through:

- **Data Validation:** Checking for missing or inconsistent values.
- **Cross-Verification:** Comparing datasets from multiple sources.
- **Using Constraints:** Enforcing data integrity rules in databases.

- **Sanity Checks:** Conducting manual verification with subject-matter experts.

7. What is ETL, and why is it important?

ETL STANDS FOR **Extract, Transform, Load**, a process used to:

- **Extract:** Retrieve data from different sources.
- **Transform:** Clean and convert data into the required format.
- **Load:** Store data into a database or warehouse for analysis. ETL is essential for ensuring reliable, structured data for business intelligence.

8. What is the difference between structured and unstructured data?

- **Structured Data:** Organized in tables (e.g., SQL databases, spreadsheets).
- **Unstructured Data:** Free-form data like emails, social media posts, images, and videos.

9. How do you handle missing data in a dataset?

TECHNIQUES FOR HANDLING missing data include:

- **Removing Missing Rows:** If the missing data is minimal and random.
- **Imputing Values:** Replacing missing values with the mean, median, or mode.
- **Using Predictive Models:** Filling missing values using regression or machine learning.

10. How do you measure the success of a data analysis

project?

SUCCESS IS MEASURED by:

- **Actionable Insights:** Does the analysis lead to tangible improvements?

- **Accuracy & Reliability:** Are the results validated and error-free?

- **Stakeholder Satisfaction:** Do the findings address business needs?

- **Efficiency Gains:** Does the project improve decision-making speed and accuracy?

11. What are KPIs, and why are they important?

KEY PERFORMANCE INDICATORS (KPIs) are measurable values that track progress toward business objectives. Examples:

- **Sales KPIs:** Revenue, conversion rate.
- **Customer KPIs:** Retention rate, Net Promoter Score (NPS).
- **Operational KPIs:** Order fulfillment time, inventory turnover.

12. How do you handle outliers in your data?

- **Identify:** Use box plots, Z-scores, or IQR methods.

- **Investigate:** Determine if they are genuine errors or meaningful insights.

- **Treat:** Remove, cap, or transform outliers if they distort analysis.

13. What is data normalization, and why is it important?

DATA NORMALIZATION organizes data to eliminate redundancy and ensure consistency. Common techniques include:

- **Min-Max Scaling:** Rescales values to a 0-1 range.

- **Z-score Standardization:** Centers data around a mean of 0 and standard deviation of 1.

- **Database Normalization:** Reduces redundancy in relational databases.

14. How do you communicate complex data insights to non-technical stakeholders?

- **Use Visualizations:** Graphs, dashboards, and charts.
- **Tell a Story:** Provide a clear narrative around the insights.
- **Avoid Jargon:** Use simple, business-friendly language.
- **Use Comparisons:** Relate insights to familiar metrics.

15. What is A/B Testing, and how is it used in data analysis?

A/B TESTING COMPARES two variations of a strategy to determine which performs better. It is widely used in:

- **Marketing:** Testing different ad creatives.
- **Web Optimization:** Comparing website designs.
- **Product Development:** Evaluating feature changes.

16. What are some challenges data analysts face?

- **Dirty Data:** Incomplete, inconsistent, or duplicated data.

- **Data Silos:** Information trapped in different systems.

- **Stakeholder Expectations:** Balancing technical limitations with business demands.

- **Changing Requirements:** Adapting to evolving business needs.

17. What is the difference between correlation and causation?

- **Correlation:** Measures the relationship between two variables.

- **Causation:** Indicates one variable directly influences another. Example: Ice cream sales and drowning incidents may be correlated due to summer heat but do not cause each other.

18. What statistical methods are commonly used in data analysis?

- **Descriptive Statistics:** Mean, median, mode, variance.
- **Inferential Statistics:** Hypothesis testing, regression analysis.
- **Probability Distributions:** Normal, binomial, Poisson distributions.

19. What role does machine learning play in data analysis?

WHILE DATA ANALYSTS focus on descriptive analysis, basic machine learning models can be used for:

- **Predictive Analysis:** Forecasting trends.
- **Clustering:** Grouping customers based on behavior.
- **Anomaly Detection:** Identifying fraudulent activities.

20. What are some best practices for working with large datasets?

- **Use Efficient Queries:** Optimize SQL queries with indexing.
- **Leverage Cloud Computing:** Utilize platforms like AWS and BigQuery.
- **Batch Processing:** Handle data in chunks to improve performance.
- **Automate Workflows:** Reduce manual errors through scripting.

Section 1: What Employers Look for in a Data Analyst

EMPLOYERS SEEK DATA analysts who can transform raw data into actionable insights. Key attributes include:

- **Technical proficiency** in SQL, Python, R, and data visualization tools.

- **Analytical thinking** to interpret and analyze data effectively.

- **Communication skills** to present findings clearly.

- **Problem-solving ability** to derive meaningful conclusions from datasets.

- **Business acumen** to understand industry-specific challenges and opportunities.

Section 2: Key Skills and Competencies

1. Data Manipulation and Analysis

- Proficiency in **SQL** for querying databases.
- Experience with **Excel, Pandas (Python), and dplyr (R)**.

2. Data Visualization

- Expertise in tools like **Tableau, Power BI, Matplotlib, and Seaborn**.
- Ability to create dashboards and reports.

3. Statistical and Analytical Skills

- Understanding of **A/B testing, regression analysis, hypothesis testing**.

4. Business Intelligence and Decision-Making

- Experience translating data insights into strategic business decisions.

5. Programming and Automation

- Scripting in **Python or R** for data processing.
- Automation of repetitive tasks using **ETL tools and workflows.**

Section 3: Tools and Technologies

1. Databases and Query Languages

- **SQL**: MySQL, PostgreSQL, Microsoft SQL Server
- **NoSQL**: MongoDB, Cassandra

2. Data Visualization Tools

- Tableau, Power BI, Looker, Google Data Studio

3. Statistical and Analytical Tools

- Python (Pandas, NumPy, Scikit-learn)
- R (ggplot2, dplyr, tidyr)

4. Big Data Technologies

- Hadoop, Spark, AWS Redshift, Google BigQuery

5. Workflow and Automation Tools

- Apache Airflow, Alteryx, KNIME

Section 4: Real-Time Interview Questions & Expert Answers

1. General Data Analyst Questions

Q1: WHAT DOES A DATA analyst do on a daily basis?

A: A data analyst collects, cleans, and interprets data to help businesses make data-driven decisions. Tasks include querying databases, performing statistical analysis, visualizing data, and presenting insights to stakeholders.

Q2: What's the difference between a data analyst and a data scientist?

A: A data analyst focuses on processing, interpreting, and reporting structured data, whereas a data scientist applies advanced machine learning and predictive modeling techniques.

Q3: How do you approach a new dataset?

A: I start by understanding the dataset's structure (columns, types, missing values), then perform exploratory data analysis (EDA) using descriptive statistics and visualizations.

2. SQL & Database Questions

Q4: WRITE AN SQL QUERY to find duplicate records in a table.

A:

```
SELECT column_name, COUNT(*)
FROM table_name
GROUP BY column_name
HAVING COUNT(*) > 1;
```

Q5: What's the difference between INNER JOIN and LEFT JOIN?

A: INNER JOIN returns only matching records from both tables, whereas LEFT JOIN returns all records from the left table and matching records from the right table (or NULL if there's no match).

3. Data Visualization Questions

Q6: HOW DO YOU DECIDE which type of chart to use?

A: I consider the data type and objective. Use a bar chart for comparisons, a line chart for trends, and a scatter plot for relationships between variables.

Q7: How would you visualize categorical data?

A: Categorical data can be visualized using bar charts, pie charts, or stacked column charts.

4. Statistics & Data Interpretation Questions

Q8: EXPLAIN THE CONCEPT of A/B testing.

A: A/B testing compares two versions of a variable (e.g., a website design) to determine which performs better using statistical significance testing.

Q9: What is p-value in hypothesis testing?

A: The p-value measures the probability that the observed result occurred by chance. A p-value below 0.05 typically indicates statistical significance.

5. Business Case & Problem-Solving Questions

Q10: HOW WOULD YOU analyze customer churn?

A: Identify factors influencing churn by segmenting customers, analyzing past behaviors, and using predictive modeling to understand patterns.

Q11: If sales dropped by 20%, how would you investigate?

A: I'd analyze sales data trends, customer behavior, external market factors, and perform cohort analysis to identify causes.

6. Programming & Automation Questions

Q12: HOW WOULD YOU clean messy data in Python?

A: Using Pandas:

```
import pandas as pd
# Drop missing values
df.dropna(inplace=True)
# Remove duplicates
df.drop_duplicates(inplace=True)
# Convert data types
df['date'] = pd.to_datetime(df['date'])
```

Q13: What are the advantages of using Python for data analysis?

A: Python offers a rich ecosystem of libraries (Pandas, NumPy, Matplotlib), automation capabilities, and integration with machine learning frameworks.

7. Scenario-Based Questions

Q14: YOU'RE GIVEN AN unstructured dataset. How do you proceed?

A: First, I examine the data structure, clean missing values, standardize formats, and apply transformations for consistency.

Q15: How would you present your findings to a non-technical stakeholder?

A: I'd use clear visualizations, storytelling techniques, and business-friendly language to communicate insights effectively.

8. Case Study Questions

Q16: SUPPOSE AN E-COMMERCE company wants to increase customer retention. What approach would you take?

A: I'd analyze past customer behavior, segment users, identify churn indicators, and propose data-driven retention strategies (e.g., personalized marketing).

Q17: If given a dataset with missing values, how would you handle it?

A: I'd assess the extent of missing data and use techniques like mean imputation, forward-fill, or machine learning-based imputation methods.

This chapter provided insights into the core skills, tools, and real-world interview questions relevant to a data analyst. Mastering these will improve your chances of acing your next data analyst interview. In the next chapter, we will dive deeper into **SQL for Data Analysis** with advanced query techniques and real-time examples.

Chapter 2: Real-Time SQL Interview Questions

Writing Complex Queries for Real-World Datasets

SQL is a fundamental skill for data analysts, and real-time interview questions often focus on writing complex queries using joins, subqueries, and window functions. This chapter covers real-time SQL interview questions along with expert answers to help you prepare for your next data analyst interview.

Question 1: How do you find the second-highest salary in a table?

Answer:

```
SELECT MAX(SALARY) AS second_highest_salary
    FROM employees
    WHERE salary < (SELECT MAX(salary) FROM employees);
```

This query finds the highest salary first and then retrieves the maximum salary that is lower than the highest salary.

Question 2: How do you retrieve duplicate records from a table?

Answer:

```
SELECT NAME, COUNT(*)
    FROM employees
```

```
GROUP BY name
HAVING COUNT(*) > 1;
```

The HAVING clause filters out records that occur more than once.

Question 3: How do you find the nth highest salary?

Answer:

```
SELECT DISTINCT SALARY FROM employees ORDER BY salary DESC
LIMIT 1 OFFSET n-1;
```

Replace n-1 with the desired ranking.

Question 4: What is the difference between INNER JOIN and LEFT JOIN?

Answer:

- INNER JOIN: Returns only matching records from both tables.
- LEFT JOIN: Returns all records from the left table and matching records from the right table; if no match is found, NULL is returned.

EXAMPLE:

```
SELECT e.name, d.department
FROM employees e
LEFT JOIN departments d ON e.department_id = d.id;
```

Question 5: How do you find employees who don't have any assigned department?

Answer:

```
SELECT E.* FROM EMPLOYEES e
LEFT JOIN departments d ON e.department_id = d.id
```

```
WHERE d.id IS NULL;
```

This query retrieves employees where no department ID matches in the departments table.

Question 6: What is a self-join? Provide an example.

Answer:

A SELF-JOIN IS A JOIN where a table is joined with itself.

```
SELECT e1.name AS employee, e2.name AS manager
FROM employees e1
JOIN employees e2 ON e1.manager_id = e2.id;
```

Question 7: How do you find the count of employees per department?

Answer:

```
SELECT DEPARTMENT_ID, COUNT(*) AS employee_count
FROM employees
GROUP BY department_id;
```

Question 8: What is a window function? Provide an example.

Answer:

A WINDOW FUNCTION PERFORMS calculations across a set of table rows related to the current row.

```
SELECT name, department_id, salary, RANK() OVER (PARTITION BY department_id ORDER BY salary DESC) AS salary_rank
FROM employees;
```

This ranks employees within each department by salary.

Question 9: How do you find consecutive records in a table?

Answer:

```
SELECT ID, NAME, SALARY, LAG(salary) OVER (ORDER BY id) AS
previous_salary
    FROM employees;
```

The LAG() function returns the previous row's salary.

Question 10: How do you find employees who joined in the last 30 days?

Answer:

```
SELECT * FROM EMPLOYEES
    WHERE join_date >= CURDATE() - INTERVAL 30 DAY;
```

Question 11: More Real-World SQL Interview Questions

1. Find the cumulative sum of salaries across employees.

```
SELECT NAME, SALARY, SUM(salary) OVER (ORDER BY id) AS
cumulative_salary FROM employees;
```

1. Find departments where the average salary is greater than $50,000.

```
SELECT department_id, AVG(salary) AS avg_salary FROM employees
GROUP BY department_id HAVING AVG(salary) > 50000;
```

1. Retrieve employees whose names start with 'A'.

```
SELECT * FROM employees WHERE name LIKE 'A%';
```

1. Find all employees with the highest salary in each department.

SELECT * FROM (SELECT name, department_id, salary, RANK() OVER (PARTITION BY department_id ORDER BY salary DESC) AS rnk FROM employees) AS temp WHERE rnk = 1;

1. Count the number of employees hired each year.

SELECT YEAR(join_date) AS year, COUNT(*) FROM employees GROUP BY year;

1. Find employees with the same salary.

SELECT salary, GROUP_CONCAT(name) FROM employees GROUP BY salary HAVING COUNT(*) > 1;

1. How do you remove duplicate rows?

DELETE e1 FROM employees e1 INNER JOIN employees e2 ON e1.name = e2.name AND e1.id > e2.id;

1. Identify gaps in employee IDs.

SELECT id+1 AS missing_id FROM employees e1 WHERE NOT EXISTS (SELECT id FROM employees e2 WHERE e2.id = e1.id+1);

1. Retrieve top 3 salaries per department.

SELECT * FROM (SELECT name, department_id, salary, DENSE_RANK() OVER (PARTITION BY department_id ORDER BY salary DESC) AS rnk FROM employees) AS temp WHERE rnk <= 3;

1. Retrieve all orders placed in the last week.

SELECT * FROM orders WHERE order_date >= CURDATE() - INTERVAL 7 DAY;

1. Find total revenue per customer.

SELECT customer_id, SUM(total_amount) FROM orders GROUP BY customer_id;

1. Identify customers who placed multiple orders on the same day.

SELECT customer_id, order_date, COUNT(*) FROM orders GROUP BY customer_id, order_date HAVING COUNT(*) > 1;

1. Find the first order for each customer.

SELECT * FROM (SELECT *, ROW_NUMBER() OVER (PARTITION BY customer_id ORDER BY order_date) AS rnk FROM orders) AS temp WHERE rnk = 1;

Structured Query Language (SQL) is the backbone of data analysis, making it a crucial skill for data analysts. SQL interviews often include real-world scenarios where candidates must demonstrate their ability to write optimized queries, avoid common mistakes, and retrieve data efficiently.

The questions are divided into two key areas:

1. **Optimizing Queries for Performance**
2. **Common SQL Mistakes and How to Avoid Them**

Each question reflects challenges faced by data analysts in real-world business environments. Mastering these questions will boost your confidence and technical skills.

Let's dive in!

Section 1: Optimizing Queries for Performance

1. What are the best practices for optimizing SQL queries?

ANSWER:

- Use **SELECT only necessary columns** instead of SELECT *.
- Use **indexes** to speed up searches.
- Optimize **JOINs** by using indexed columns.

- Avoid **correlated subqueries**, prefer **JOINs**.
- Use **EXPLAIN PLAN** to analyze query performance.

---

2. How do indexes improve query performance?

ANSWER:

Indexes store sorted data, making lookups faster. They reduce the number of rows scanned, improving WHERE, JOIN, and ORDER BY performance. However, excessive indexing can slow down inserts and updates.

---

3. What is the difference between clustered and non-clustered indexes?

ANSWER:

- **Clustered Index:** Sorts and stores data in order. Only one per table.
- **Non-Clustered Index:** Stores a separate structure for indexing. Multiple allowed per table.

Example:

sql

```
CREATE CLUSTERED INDEX idx_employee ON Employee(EmployeeID);
CREATE NONCLUSTERED INDEX idx_name ON Employee(LastName);
```

---

4. What is an execution plan, and how can it help optimize queries?

ANSWER:

An execution plan shows how SQL executes a query. It helps identify bottlenecks, inefficient JOINs, and missing indexes. Use:

sql

```
EXPLAIN ANALYZE SELECT * FROM Orders WHERE OrderDate > '2024-01-01';
```

5. How does indexing affect INSERT, UPDATE, and DELETE operations?

ANSWER:

Indexes speed up SELECT queries but slow down INSERT, UPDATE, and DELETE operations because the index must be updated along with the data.

6. When should you use partitioning in SQL?

ANSWER:

Use partitioning for large tables to improve query performance. It helps when querying a specific partition rather than scanning the entire table.

Example:

sql

```
CREATE TABLE Orders (
OrderID INT,
OrderDate DATE
) PARTITION BY RANGE (YEAR(OrderDate));
```

7. How do CTEs (Common Table Expressions) improve query performance?

ANSWER:

CTEs improve readability and avoid redundant subqueries. They can optimize recursive queries.

Example:

sql

```
WITH Sales AS (
SELECT CustomerID, SUM(Amount) AS TotalSales
FROM Orders
GROUP BY CustomerID
)
```

```sql
SELECT * FROM Sales WHERE TotalSales > 1000;
```

8. What is the impact of using DISTINCT in a query?

ANSWER:

DISTINCT removes duplicates but can be slow due to sorting. Use only when necessary.

Example:

```sql
SELECT DISTINCT Country FROM Customers;
```

9. How do you optimize queries using indexing strategies?

ANSWER:

- Use **covering indexes** (include all required columns).
- Prefer **multi-column indexes** for filtering.
- Avoid indexing on columns with low cardinality (e.g., Boolean values).

10. What is database denormalization, and how does it affect performance?

ANSWER:

Denormalization reduces JOINs by storing redundant data, improving read performance but increasing storage and update costs.

Section 2: Common SQL Mistakes and How to Avoid Them

11. What are the most common SQL mistakes data analysts make?

ANSWER:

- Using SELECT * instead of specific columns.

- Not using indexes for large datasets.
- Forgetting to use GROUP BY with aggregate functions.
- Using HAVING instead of WHERE for filtering.

---

*12. Why should you avoid using SELECT ?

ANSWER:

Fetching unnecessary columns increases memory usage and slows performance.

Example:

sql

```
SELECT Name, Age FROM Employees;—Instead of SELECT * FROM Employees;
```

---

13. How can NULL values impact SQL queries?

ANSWER:

NULL values can cause unexpected results in aggregates and comparisons. Always use COALESCE() or IS NULL checks.

Example:

sql

```
SELECT COALESCE(Salary, 0) FROM Employees;
```

---

14. What happens if you forget the WHERE clause in DELETE or UPDATE statements?

ANSWER:

Forgetting WHERE can delete or update all rows.

Example:

sql

```
UPDATE Employees SET Salary = 50000 WHERE EmployeeID = 1;
DELETE FROM Employees WHERE EmployeeID = 2;
```

---

15. How do you prevent SQL injection attacks?

ANSWER:

Use **prepared statements** instead of dynamic SQL.

Example:

```sql
PREPARE stmt FROM 'SELECT * FROM Users WHERE Username = ?';
EXECUTE stmt USING 'john_doe';
```

---

16. What is the difference between INNER JOIN and OUTER JOIN?

ANSWER:

- **INNER JOIN:** Returns only matching rows.
- **OUTER JOIN:** Includes unmatched rows (LEFT, RIGHT, FULL).

Example:

SELECT * FROM Customers INNER JOIN Orders ON Customers.ID = Orders.CustomerID;

---

17. Why is it important to use appropriate data types?

ANSWER:

Incorrect data types lead to inefficient queries and storage issues. Use VARCHAR(100) instead of TEXT for short strings.

---

18. How do you handle duplicate data in SQL?

ANSWER:

Use DISTINCT, GROUP BY, or ROW_NUMBER().

Example:

SELECT DISTINCT Email FROM Users;

---

19. What is the impact of using ORDER BY without an index?

ANSWER:

Sorting large datasets without an index leads to slow queries.

Example:

```
CREATE INDEX idx_lastname ON Employees(LastName);
SELECT * FROM Employees ORDER BY LastName;
```

---

20. What is the difference between HAVING and WHERE?

ANSWER:

- WHERE filters before grouping.
- HAVING filters after aggregation.

Example:

```
SELECT Department, AVG(Salary) FROM Employees GROUP BY Department HAVING AVG(Salary) > 50000;
```

Mastering SQL is essential for data analysts, and avoiding common pitfalls while optimizing queries can significantly impact performance. By understanding **real-time interview questions**, you'll be well-equipped to tackle SQL-related challenges in any data analyst interview.

Practice these concepts to improve your SQL skills and enhance your chances of success in interviews.

Chapter 3: Practical Data Visualization & Reporting Scenarios

Section 1: Analyzing and Presenting Data Using Tableau, Power BI, and Excel

In this section, we cover real-time interview questions asked in data analyst interviews, specifically focusing on Tableau, Power BI, and Excel. These questions will test your ability to analyze and present data effectively using these tools.

Question 1: How do you handle large datasets in Tableau without performance issues?

ANSWER:

To optimize performance in Tableau with large datasets:

- Use **Extracts** instead of Live Connections when possible.
- Optimize **calculated fields** by reducing unnecessary computations.
- Use **data aggregation** and summarization to limit the number of rows.
- Utilize **indexed tables** and performance-optimized SQL queries.
- Reduce the use of complex joins and filters, replacing them with **context filters** when necessary.

Question 2: How do you create a dynamic dashboard in Power BI?

ANSWER:

A dynamic dashboard in Power BI can be created by:

- Using **slicers and filters** to allow users to interact with the data.
- Implementing **measures using DAX** (e.g., CALCULATE, FILTER, SWITCH) for dynamic calculations.
- Utilizing **Bookmarks and Buttons** to create toggle views.
- Incorporating **drill-through pages** for detailed insights.
- Implementing **custom visuals** when standard ones don't meet requirements.

Question 3: What are context filters in Tableau, and why are they important?

ANSWER:

Context filters are used to define a subset of data that other filters will act upon. They improve performance by:

- Reducing the number of records processed by other filters.
- Helping to set dependent filtering in dashboards.
- Enhancing query execution speed by optimizing underlying SQL queries.

Example: If you filter sales data for a specific region using a context filter, all other filters (e.g., product category) will apply only to that region, improving performance and accuracy.

Question 4: How do you optimize DAX performance in Power BI?

ANSWER:

DAX performance can be optimized by:

- Avoiding **row-by-row operations** (FILTER, SUMX) when columnar operations (SUM, COUNT) suffice.
- Using **variables** (VAR) to store values and reduce redundant calculations.
- Reducing **cardinality** by optimizing data types and aggregations.
- Leveraging **SUMMARIZECOLUMNS** instead of SUMMARIZE for better efficiency.
- Avoiding complex calculated columns in large datasets.

Question 5: What are calculated fields and table calculations in Tableau?

ANSWER:

- **Calculated Fields:** Created at the data source level, allowing custom expressions (e.g., IF, CASE, SUM).
- **Table Calculations:** Computed at the visualization level, applying functions like RANK(), WINDOW_SUM(), or RUNNING_AVG().

Example:

A **calculated field** can be used to segment customers (IF [Sales] > 1000 THEN "High Value" ELSE "Low Value"), whereas a **table calculation** might compute cumulative sales across time (RUNNING_SUM([Sales])).

Question 6: How do you use row-level security (RLS) in Power BI?

ANSWER:

RLS in Power BI restricts data access based on user roles:

- Define **roles in Power BI Desktop** using FILTER() in DAX.
- Apply roles to datasets using **Manage Roles** in the Model tab.
- Publish to Power BI Service and assign users to roles in **Security Settings.**

Example:
A sales manager should only see data for their region:
[Region] = USERPRINCIPALNAME()

Question 7: How do you use pivot tables in Excel for data analysis?

ANSWER:

Pivot tables summarize large datasets efficiently by:

- Dragging fields into **Rows, Columns, Values,** and **Filters.**
- Using **Calculated Fields** to create new metrics.
- Applying **slicers and timelines** for interactive filtering.
- Summarizing data using **SUM, COUNT, AVERAGE, MIN, MAX.**

Section 2: Real-World Chart Selection Challenges

THIS SECTION DISCUSSES common real-world challenges in choosing the right charts for different data scenarios.

Question 8: When should you use a bar chart instead of a pie chart?

ANSWER:

A bar chart is preferred when:

- Comparing multiple categories clearly.
- Data labels in a pie chart would be cluttered.
- Precise numerical differences are important.

Example: A **bar chart** is better for comparing sales across five regions than a **pie chart**, which may become difficult to interpret with too many categories.

Question 9: What is the best way to visualize time series data?

ANSWER:

For time series data:

- **Line charts** are best for trends over time.
- **Area charts** work well for cumulative trends.
- **Bar charts** can show monthly/yearly comparisons.

Example: **Stock price fluctuations** are best shown using a line chart.

Question 10: What type of chart is ideal for showing relationships between two numeric variables?

ANSWER:

A **scatter plot** is ideal, as it:

- Shows **correlations** (e.g., sales vs. advertising spend).
- Identifies **outliers**.
- Displays **clusters and trends**.

Question 11: How do you decide when to use a heatmap?

ANSWER:

A **heatmap** is useful when visualizing data density or relationships in a matrix format.

Example: In a **customer churn analysis**, a heatmap can highlight which customer segments are more likely to leave.

Question 12: What is a waterfall chart, and when should you use it?

ANSWER:

A waterfall chart shows **incremental changes** over time, useful for financial reports.

Example: **Profit and loss statements** benefit from waterfall charts by showing revenue, costs, and net income changes.

Question 13: When should you use a bullet chart?

ANSWER:

Bullet charts are great for **goal vs. actual performance** comparisons.

Example: If you need to compare a company's **monthly revenue target** vs. actual revenue, a bullet chart provides clarity.

Question 14: What are the limitations of a pie chart?

ANSWER:

- Difficult to compare **multiple categories.**
- Hard to interpret when values are similar.
- Not ideal for **trend analysis.**

Example: Instead of a pie chart, a **stacked bar chart** is often better for comparing proportions over time.

Question 15: How do you create an interactive dashboard in Tableau?

ANSWER:

- Use **dashboard actions** to allow interactions.
- Implement **parameters** for dynamic user inputs.
- Utilize **filters and highlights** for a better experience.

Example: Clicking on a **region in a map** updates sales details below it.

Section 3: Case Study – Creating an Executive Dashboard

IN ANY DATA-DRIVEN organization, executive dashboards play a crucial role in providing leadership teams with insights that support strategic decision-making. These dashboards need to be concise, visually appealing, and packed with meaningful KPIs (Key Performance Indicators).

In this section, we will explore a real-time interview scenario where a candidate is asked to design an executive dashboard. We will cover 10 common interview questions related to dashboard design, best practices, and implementation strategies. Each question is accompanied by a structured answer that highlights the key concepts expected in an interview setting.

Q1: What are the key components of an effective executive dashboard?

ANSWER:

An effective executive dashboard includes:

1. **Key Metrics & KPIs:** Metrics should be aligned with business objectives.
2. **Data Summarization:** High-level insights with drill-down capabilities.
3. **Visual Clarity:** Use appropriate charts and avoid clutter.
4. **Interactivity:** Filters and segmentation for detailed analysis.
5. **Real-time or Scheduled Data Refresh:** Ensures up-to-date insights.

Q2: How do you decide which KPIs to include in an executive dashboard?

ANSWER:

- Understand business objectives and align KPIs accordingly.
- Prioritize metrics that drive decision-making.
- Focus on **SMART KPIs** (Specific, Measurable, Achievable, Relevant, Time-bound).
- Avoid vanity metrics and emphasize performance indicators that impact revenue, customer satisfaction, or efficiency.

Q3: What tools would you use to build an executive dashboard, and why?

ANSWER:

Common tools include:

- **Tableau & Power BI:** Excellent for visualization, interactivity, and real-time data connectivity.
- **Google Data Studio:** Free tool for quick dashboard creation.
- **Excel:** Useful for static reports and quick data analysis.
- **Looker & Qlik Sense:** For advanced data modeling and interactive reporting.

The choice of tool depends on organizational needs, budget, and data complexity.

Q4: How do you ensure an executive dashboard remains relevant over time?

ANSWER:

- Conduct periodic reviews with stakeholders.
- Implement **automated alerts** for KPI thresholds.
- Use adaptive design principles to accommodate business changes.
- Keep dashboards simple and avoid unnecessary complexity.

Q5: What are the best practices for designing an effective dashboard layout?

ANSWER:

- **Top-left priority:** Place the most important KPIs in the top-left corner.
- **Minimalist approach:** Avoid excessive text and unnecessary visuals.
- **Color consistency:** Use a uniform color scheme with meaningful contrasts.
- **Responsive design:** Ensure compatibility across devices.
- **Logical grouping:** Organize KPIs in a structured manner.

Q6: How would you handle data discrepancies in an executive dashboard?

ANSWER:

- Cross-check data sources for inconsistencies.
- Validate ETL (Extract, Transform, Load) processes.
- Implement data governance policies.
- Communicate data limitations transparently with stakeholders.

Q7: How do you incorporate interactivity into an executive dashboard?

ANSWER:

- Use filters for date, region, or product categories.

- Enable drill-down features for in-depth analysis.
- Include dynamic trend lines and comparisons.

Q8: What are some common KPIs used in an executive dashboard?

ANSWER:

- **Financial KPIs:** Revenue, profit margins, expenses.
- **Operational KPIs:** Efficiency ratios, production rates.
- **Customer KPIs:** Retention rate, Net Promoter Score (NPS).
- **Marketing KPIs:** Conversion rates, campaign ROI.

Q9: How do you deal with stakeholders who request frequent dashboard changes?

ANSWER:

- Set clear expectations on dashboard functionality.
- Implement a structured **change request process**.
- Educate stakeholders on the cost and feasibility of changes.
- Offer a self-service BI solution where possible.

Q10: How would you present the insights from an executive dashboard to a leadership team?

ANSWER:

- Start with **key takeaways** and trends.
- Highlight **business impact** rather than just numbers.
- Use storytelling techniques to explain insights.
- Be prepared with recommendations based on the data.

Section 4: Common Visualization Pitfalls

CREATING DATA VISUALIZATIONS is not just about presenting data; it's about ensuring that the data tells the right story. Many analysts, especially beginners, make visualization mistakes that mislead stakeholders. This section highlights 10 common pitfalls in data visualization, with corresponding interview questions and answers to help you navigate these challenges.

Q11: What are the most common mistakes in data visualization?

ANSWER:

1. **Overloading dashboards with too much data.**
2. **Using the wrong chart type for the data.**
3. **Ignoring audience context and preferences.**
4. **Poor color choices leading to misinterpretation.**
5. **Lack of clear labeling or misleading axis scaling.**

Q12: How do you choose the right visualization type?

ANSWER:

- **Bar charts:** Comparisons across categories.
- **Line charts:** Trends over time.
- **Pie charts:** Proportional data (use sparingly).
- **Heatmaps:** Patterns in large datasets.

Always consider **data relationships** and the audience's ability to interpret the chart correctly.

Q13: Why should pie charts be avoided in most cases?

ANSWER:

- Difficult to compare slices accurately.
- Limited space for labels.

- Misleading when there are too many categories.

Use a **bar chart** instead for clearer comparisons.

Q14: What are the dangers of truncating the Y-axis in a chart?

ANSWER:

- Can exaggerate differences between data points.
- Misleads the audience by distorting proportionality.
- Always start the Y-axis at zero unless an exception is justified.

Q15: How do you ensure your visualizations are accessible to all users?

ANSWER:

- Use colorblind-friendly palettes.
- Provide alternative text for visuals.
- Ensure charts are readable on mobile devices.

Q16: What are the consequences of using too many colors in a visualization?

ANSWER:

- Causes cognitive overload.
- Makes it hard to identify key insights.
- Stick to a **consistent color scheme** with minimal variations.

Q17: How do you deal with missing data in a visualization?

ANSWER:

- Use placeholders or explanatory notes.

- Apply interpolation where appropriate.
- Offer a "**No Data Available**" message instead of misleading visuals.

Q18: What role does storytelling play in data visualization?

ANSWER:

- Helps stakeholders **understand** and **remember** insights.
- Provides context to data trends.
- Ensures data-driven decision-making is **actionable**.

Q19: What's the biggest challenge in designing a dashboard for a non-technical audience?

ANSWER:

- Avoiding jargon-heavy metrics.
- Ensuring simplicity while maintaining depth.
- Using **self-explanatory visuals** with minimal required interpretation.

Q20: How do you validate the accuracy of a visualization?

ANSWER:

- Cross-check with raw data and summary statistics.
- Validate with SMEs (Subject Matter Experts).
- Ensure ETL processes are correctly implemented.

By mastering these real-time interview questions, you'll be better prepared to tackle data analyst interviews confidently. The key to success is not only understanding the technical aspects of visualization but also communicating insights effectively.

With a well-structured executive dashboard and awareness of common visualization pitfalls, you can ensure your reporting is impactful and reliable.

Chapter 4: Real-Time Data Cleaning & Preprocessing Challenges

Section 1: Handling Missing Values and Inconsistent Data

In data analysis, handling missing values and inconsistent data is one of the most critical preprocessing steps. Real-time interview questions often test a candidate's ability to deal with incomplete datasets efficiently. Below are 15 real-time interview questions with expert answers focused on missing values and inconsistent data.

Question 1: What are the different types of missing data, and how do you handle them?

ANSWER:

Missing data can be categorized into:

- **Missing Completely at Random (MCAR):** No pattern exists in missing values.
- **Missing at Random (MAR):** The missingness depends on observed data but not on the missing values themselves.
- **Missing Not at Random (MNAR):** The missing values depend on unobserved data.

Handling techniques include:

- **Dropping missing values** (if they are few and non-essential).

• **Imputation** using mean, median, mode, or predictive models like k-NN.

• **Using algorithms that handle missing values,** like decision trees or XGBoost.

Question 2: When should you remove missing data instead of imputing it?

ANSWER:

Removing missing data is preferred when:

1. The percentage of missing values is small (e.g., <5%).
2. The missing data is not systematically biased.
3. The missing column is not critical for the analysis.

If removing leads to data loss or bias, imputation is a better choice.

Question 3: What are the different imputation techniques used in real-time projects?

ANSWER:

1. **Mean, Median, Mode Imputation** – Simple but may not work well for skewed distributions.
2. **Forward Fill and Backward Fill** – Used in time-series data.
3. **K-Nearest Neighbors (KNN) Imputation** – Uses similarities to fill missing values.
4. **Regression Imputation** – Predicts missing values based on other variables.
5. **Multiple Imputation** – Generates multiple datasets with different imputations and averages the results.

Question 4: How do you detect and handle inconsistent data in a dataset?

ANSWER:

- **Detection:**
  - Check for duplicate records.
  - Identify conflicting information (e.g., mismatched categories, typos).
  - Use summary statistics (mean, min, max) to spot anomalies.
- **Handling:**
  - Standardizing formats (e.g., date formats, text cases).
  - Correcting incorrect spellings and category mismatches.
  - Removing duplicate entries.

Question 5: How do you handle missing categorical data?

ANSWER:

Options include:

1. **Mode imputation** (replacing missing values with the most frequent category).
2. **Using 'Unknown' or 'Other' category** to avoid information loss.
3. **Predicting missing values** using machine learning models.

Question 6: How do you deal with outliers in a dataset?

ANSWER:

1. **Z-score or IQR method** to identify and remove extreme values.
2. **Transformation techniques** (e.g., log transformation) to normalize data.
3. **Capping and flooring** – Setting upper and lower bounds.

Question 7: How do you handle mixed data types in a single column?

ANSWER:

- Convert all values to a consistent format (e.g., text to numerical).
- Use regular expressions to extract correct values.
- Drop or split columns if necessary.

Question 8: How do you validate data after cleaning?

ANSWER:

- **Check for duplicates, missing values, and outliers.**
- **Run summary statistics.**
- **Use data visualization to inspect trends and distributions.**

Section 2: Cleaning Datasets Using SQL, Python, or Excel

BELOW ARE 15 REAL-TIME interview questions focused on data cleaning using different tools.

Question 9: How do you remove duplicates in SQL?

ANSWER:

```
DELETE FROM table_name
WHERE id NOT IN (
SELECT MIN(id)
FROM table_name
GROUP BY column_name
);
```

This query retains the first occurrence and removes duplicates.

Question 10: How do you handle NULL values in SQL?

ANSWER:

Replace NULLs with default values:

SELECT COALESCE(column_name, 'default_value') FROM table_name;

•

Filter out NULL values:

SELECT * FROM table_name WHERE column_name IS NOT NULL;

•

Question 11: How do you replace missing values in Pandas?

ANSWER:

df['column_name'].fillna(df['column_name'].mean(), inplace=True)

This replaces missing values with the mean.

Question 12: How do you remove special characters from a column in Pandas?

ANSWER:

df['column_name'] = df['column_name'].str.replace('[^a-zA-Z0-9]', '', regex=True)

Question 13: How do you split a column into multiple columns in Pandas?

ANSWER:

df[['first_name', 'last_name']] = df['full_name'].str.split(' ', expand=True)

Question 14: How do you identify outliers in Excel?

ANSWER:

Use the **=QUARTILE.EXC(range, 1)** and **=QUARTILE.EXC(range, 3)** functions to calculate Q1 and Q3, then find outliers using the IQR method.

Question 15: How do you remove duplicates in Excel?

ANSWER:

- Use **Data > Remove Duplicates** feature.

Use the formula:

```
=COUNTIF(A:A, A2)>1
```

- Then filter and remove duplicates.

Question 16: How do you use SQL to find missing values in a table?

ANSWER:

```
SELECT * FROM table_name WHERE column_name IS NULL;
```

Question 17: How do you replace NULL values in SQL dynamically?

ANSWER:

```
UPDATE table_name
SET column_name = COALESCE(column_name, 'default_value');
```

Question 18: How do you handle date formatting issues in SQL?

ANSWER:

```
SELECT TO_DATE(date_column, 'YYYY-MM-DD') FROM table_name;
```

Question 19: How do you drop rows with missing values in Pandas?

ANSWER:

```
df.dropna(inplace=True)
```

Question 20: How do you standardize text data in Pandas?

ANSWER:

```
df['column_name'] = df['column_name'].str.lower().str.strip()
```

Question 21: How do you merge two datasets using SQL?

ANSWER:

```
SELECT * FROM table1
JOIN table2
ON table1.id = table2.id;
```

Question 22: How do you use regular expressions to clean data in Pandas?

ANSWER:

```
df['column_name'] = df['column_name'].str.replace(r'\d+', '', regex=True)
```

Question 23: How do you clean phone numbers in Excel?

ANSWER:

Use the formula:

```
=SUBSTITUTE(A2, "-", "")
```

To remove dashes.

Question 24: How do you find and replace values in Pandas?

ANSWER:

```
df['column_name'] = df['column_name'].replace('old_value', 'new_value')
```

Section 3: Case Study – Fixing a Messy Dataset Before Analysis

IN REAL-WORLD DATA analysis, raw data is often messy, inconsistent, and full of missing values. Before conducting any meaningful analysis, data analysts must clean and preprocess the dataset. This section provides a case study of how a real-world messy dataset is cleaned and prepared for analysis. The process includes identifying issues, handling missing values, removing duplicates, dealing with inconsistent data formats, and ensuring data accuracy.

Case Study: Cleaning a Customer Sales Dataset

Step 1: Understanding the Dataset

IMAGINE YOU ARE WORKING for an e-commerce company, and you receive a raw dataset containing customer sales records. The dataset includes the following columns:

- **Customer_ID** (Unique identifier for customers)
- **Name** (Customer's name)
- **Email** (Customer's email)
- **Purchase_Date** (Date of purchase)
- **Amount_Spent** (Total amount spent)
- **Product_Category** (Category of the purchased item)
- **Payment_Method** (Mode of payment)

Step 2: Identifying Data Issues

UPON AN INITIAL REVIEW, you find the following issues in the dataset:

1. **Missing values**: Some rows have missing emails or purchase dates.
2. **Duplicate records**: Some customers appear multiple times with the same details.
3. **Inconsistent formatting**: Dates are stored in different formats (MM/DD/YYYY, DD-MM-YYYY, etc.).
4. **Spelling errors**: Some product categories have inconsistent spelling (e.g., "Electronics," "Eletronics").
5. **Outliers**: Some entries show abnormally high spending (e.g., $1,000,000).
6. **Incorrect email formats**: Some emails are missing "@" or have typos

like "gmail.con" instead of "gmail.com".

Step 3: Cleaning and Fixing the Dataset

Handling Missing Values

- If the **email** column is missing, we check if the same customer appears elsewhere with a valid email. If not, we remove the entry.

- If the **purchase date** is missing, we attempt to retrieve it from other records or drop the entry if it's essential.

Removing Duplicates

- Identify duplicate entries by checking Customer_ID and Name.
- Keep the latest transaction and remove the older ones.

Standardizing Formats

- Convert all **dates** to a single format (e.g., YYYY-MM-DD).
- Standardize text entries (e.g., "Eletronics" → "Electronics").

Handling Outliers

- Analyze the distribution of **Amount_Spent** using statistical methods (e.g., interquartile range, Z-score).

- Flag values beyond acceptable limits and validate them.

Fixing Incorrect Email Formats

- Use regex patterns to identify incorrect emails.
- Correct common errors (e.g., "gmail.con" → "gmail.com").

Section 4: Data Transformation Techniques in Real-World Scenarios

AFTER CLEANING THE dataset, we must transform it to prepare for analysis. Data transformation involves converting raw data into a structured format suitable for visualization, modeling, and decision-making.

Common Data Transformation Techniques

1. Normalization and Standardization

- Used when working with numerical data.
- **Normalization**: Scales values between 0 and 1. Useful for machine learning models.
- **Standardization**: Converts values to have a mean of 0 and a standard deviation of 1.

2. Encoding Categorical Data

- **Label Encoding**: Converts categories into numerical values (e.g., Male = 0, Female = 1).
- **One-Hot Encoding**: Creates separate binary columns for each category.

3. Aggregation

- Summarizes data at a higher level. Example:
    - Instead of storing every transaction, we aggregate data by **total monthly sales per customer**.

4. Parsing and Extracting Information

- Splitting full names into first and last names.
- Extracting year and month from date columns.

5. Handling Skewed Data

- If numeric data is highly skewed, apply log transformation to normalize distribution.

6. Data Binning

- Groups numerical values into bins (e.g., Age 18-25, 26-35).

Real-Time Interview Questions & Expert Answers

HERE ARE **real-time interview questions** related to **data cleaning and transformation**, along with **expert answers** that will help you prepare.

General Data Cleaning Questions

1. HOW DO YOU HANDLE missing data in a dataset?
Missing data can be handled in several ways:

- Remove rows with missing values if they are insignificant.
- Use statistical methods like mean, median, or mode imputation.
- Apply predictive models to estimate missing values.

2. What are some common data quality issues in real-world datasets?

- Missing values
- Duplicates
- Inconsistent formats
- Outliers
- Incorrectly labeled data

3. How do you detect and remove duplicate records?

- Use **Pandas .duplicated()** function to identify duplicate rows.
- Remove duplicates based on a unique identifier.

4. How do you standardize text data?

- Convert all text to **lowercase.**
- Remove extra **spaces, special characters, and typos.**
- Use a **dictionary** for common spelling corrections.

Handling Outliers and Anomalies

5. WHAT METHODS DO you use to detect outliers?

- **Boxplots and histograms** to visualize data.
- **Z-score** (values beyond ±3 standard deviations).
- **Interquartile Range (IQR)** method.

6. What steps do you take when you detect outliers?

- Validate if they are errors.
- Transform data using log scaling if necessary.
- Remove extreme outliers if justified.

Data Transformation Questions

7. WHAT IS THE DIFFERENCE between normalization and standardization?

- **Normalization** scales values between 0 and 1.

- **Standardization** transforms data to have a mean of 0 and a standard deviation of 1.

8. Why do we use one-hot encoding instead of label encoding?

- One-hot encoding prevents the model from assuming an ordinal relationship between categories.

9. How do you transform a skewed dataset?

- Use **log transformation** or **Box-Cox transformation.**

Practical Case-Based Questions

10. IF YOUR DATASET has mixed date formats, how do you fix them?

- Convert all dates to **YYYY-MM-DD** using Pandas pd.to_datetime().

11. You find inconsistent categorical labels in a dataset. How do you standardize them?

- Use a **mapping dictionary** to convert similar categories into a standard format.

12. Your dataset contains missing customer age values. How do you handle this?

- Use **median age** for missing values.
- Predict missing values using **regression models.**

Advanced Questions

13. HOW DO YOU HANDLE data with different time zones?

- Convert all timestamps to a **single standard time zone** (e.g., UTC).

14. How do you ensure data integrity when merging multiple datasets?

- Check for **duplicate records, conflicting values, and missing keys.**

15. How do you deal with high-cardinality categorical variables?

- Use **target encoding** or **dimensionality reduction techniques.**

Data cleaning and transformation are critical in ensuring high-quality analysis. Mastering these techniques will help you excel in real-world scenarios and impress interviewers with practical solutions.

Chapter 5: Python for Data Analysis – Real-Time Applications

Section 1: Writing Scripts to Analyze Real Datasets

Python is one of the most widely used programming languages for data analysis. In interviews, candidates are often tested on their ability to write scripts to manipulate, clean, and analyze real datasets. Below are real-time interview questions with expert answers.

Q1: How do you read a large CSV file efficiently in Python?

ANSWER:

Using **pandas**, you can efficiently read large CSV files by specifying parameters like chunksize or using **Dask** for parallel computation.

Example:

```
import pandas as pd
chunk_size = 10000 # Process 10,000 rows at a time
for chunk in pd.read_csv("large_dataset.csv", chunksize=chunk_size):
print(chunk.head())
```

This approach prevents memory overflow and allows processing in smaller batches.

Q2: How do you handle missing data in a dataset?

ANSWER:

You can handle missing values using Pandas' .dropna() or .fillna() methods.

Example:

```
df.dropna(inplace=True) # Remove missing values
```

df.fillna(df.mean(), inplace=True) # Replace missing values with the column mean

Using fillna() ensures data consistency without removing valuable records.

Q3: How do you identify duplicate records in a dataset?

ANSWER:

You can use the .duplicated() method in Pandas.

duplicates = df[df.duplicated()]

print(duplicates)

df.drop_duplicates(inplace=True) # Remove duplicates

This helps ensure data integrity before analysis.

Q4: How can you filter rows based on conditions?

ANSWER:

Use Boolean indexing to filter rows in Pandas.

Example:

filtered_df = df[df["age"] > 30] # Select rows where age is greater than 30

This method allows dynamic filtering based on dataset requirements.

Q5: How do you group data and calculate aggregated statistics?

ANSWER:

Using the .groupby() function:

df.groupby("department")["salary"].mean()

This groups data by **department** and calculates the average salary.

Q6: How do you merge two datasets in Python?

ANSWER:

Use merge() to combine datasets on a common column.

Example:

merged_df = df1.merge(df2, on="employee_id", how="inner")

Different join types (inner, left, right, outer) control how data is combined.

Q7: How can you pivot a dataset in Pandas?

ANSWER:

Using .pivot_table():

```
df.pivot_table(values="sales", index="region", columns="year", aggfunc="sum")
```

This restructures data for better analysis.

Q8: How do you remove outliers from a dataset?

ANSWER:

Using the **Interquartile Range (IQR)** method:

```
Q1 = df["salary"].quantile(0.25)
Q3 = df["salary"].quantile(0.75)
IQR = Q3 - Q1
df_filtered = df[(df["salary"] > (Q1 - 1.5 * IQR)) & (df["salary"] < (Q3 + 1.5 * IQR))]
```

This helps maintain accurate insights by removing extreme values.

Q9: How do you efficiently count unique values in a column?

ANSWER:

Use .nunique():

```
df["category"].nunique()
```

This is faster and memory-efficient for large datasets.

Q10: How do you write a function to automate data cleaning?

ANSWER:

```
def clean_data(df):
df.drop_duplicates(inplace=True)
df.fillna(df.median(), inplace=True)
return df
df = clean_data(df)
```

Reusable functions improve data pipeline efficiency.

Section 2: Pandas and NumPy in Action

NUMPY AND PANDAS ARE fundamental libraries for data manipulation. Below are real-time interview questions related to their usage.

Q11: What are the key differences between NumPy and Pandas?

ANSWER:

- **NumPy:** Works with arrays, fast mathematical operations.
- **Pandas:** Built on NumPy, provides DataFrames for structured data manipulation.

Q12: How do you create a NumPy array?

ANSWER:

```
import numpy as np
arr = np.array([1, 2, 3, 4, 5])
```

This is more efficient than Python lists.

Q13: How do you generate a range of numbers in NumPy?

ANSWER:

Using arange():

```
np.arange(1, 10, 2) # Generates [1, 3, 5, 7, 9]
```

Efficiently creates numerical sequences.

Q14: How do you reshape a NumPy array?

ANSWER:

```
arr.reshape(3, 2) # Reshape into 3 rows, 2 columns
```

This is useful for matrix manipulations.

Q15: How do you calculate the mean and standard deviation in NumPy?

ANSWER:

np.mean(arr), np.std(arr)

These functions are optimized for numerical computations.

Q16: How do you convert a NumPy array into a Pandas DataFrame?

ANSWER:

df = pd.DataFrame(arr, columns=["values"])

This allows seamless transition between libraries.

Q17: How do you select specific columns in Pandas?

ANSWER:

df[["column1", "column2"]]

Efficient for working with large datasets.

Q18: How do you apply a function to a Pandas column?

ANSWER:

Using .apply():

df["salary"] = df["salary"].apply(lambda x: x * 1.1)

Great for feature engineering and transformations.

Q19: How do you handle categorical data in Pandas?

ANSWER:

Use **one-hot encoding** or .astype("category"):

df["category"] = df["category"].astype("category")

Improves memory efficiency.

Q20: How do you sort a DataFrame?

ANSWER:

df.sort_values(by="age", ascending=False)

Used to organize data for analysis.

Q21: How do you concatenate two Pandas DataFrames?

ANSWER:

df = pd.concat([df1, df2], axis=0)

Merges datasets row-wise.

Q22: How do you calculate correlation between two columns?

ANSWER:

df["col1"].corr(df["col2"])

This helps in identifying relationships between variables.

Q23: What is vectorization in NumPy?

ANSWER:

It allows operations without explicit loops, improving efficiency.

Example:

arr * 2 # Each element is multiplied by 2

Q24: How do you find unique values in a NumPy array?

ANSWER:

np.unique(arr)

Useful for categorical data processing.

Q25: How do you save and load a Pandas DataFrame?

ANSWER:

df.to_csv("data.csv", index=False)

df = pd.read_csv("data.csv")

Ensures efficient data storage and retrieval.

Section 3: Case Study – Automating Data Extraction and Transformation

AUTOMATION PLAYS A crucial role in data analysis, reducing manual effort, improving efficiency, and ensuring accuracy. Companies expect data analysts to be proficient in **automating data extraction, transformation, and loading (ETL) using Python**.

Below are **real interview questions** focusing on data automation, followed by short but effective answers.

---

1. How do you automate data extraction from a database using Python?

ANSWER: You can automate data extraction using Python libraries such as **pandas, SQLAlchemy, or pyodbc**. Example:

```
import pandas as pd
from sqlalchemy import create_engine
engine = create_engine('mysql+pymysql://user:password@host/db_name')
query = "SELECT * FROM sales_data"
df = pd.read_sql(query, engine)
df.to_csv('sales_data.csv', index=False)
```

This extracts data from a MySQL database and saves it as a CSV file.

---

2. What are some common Python libraries for web scraping?

ANSWER: The most commonly used Python libraries for web scraping include:

- **BeautifulSoup** (for parsing HTML and XML)
- **Scrapy** (for large-scale scraping)
- **Selenium** (for scraping dynamic web pages)
- **Requests** (for sending HTTP requests)

---

3. How can you schedule an automated data extraction job in Python?

ANSWER: You can use **Windows Task Scheduler (Windows)** or **cron jobs (Linux/Mac)**. Alternatively, Python's **schedule** library:

```
import schedule
import time
def extract_data():
print("Extracting data...")
schedule.every().day.at("10:00").do(extract_data)
while True:
schedule.run_pending()
time.sleep(1)
```

---

4. How do you automate data extraction from an API?

ANSWER: Use the **requests** library:

```
import requests
url = "https://api.example.com/data"
headers = {"Authorization": "Bearer YOUR_TOKEN"}
response = requests.get(url, headers=headers)
if response.status_code == 200:
data = response.json()
print(data)
```

This fetches JSON data from an API.

---

5. How do you extract data from an Excel file automatically?

ANSWER: Use **pandas** to read Excel files:

```
import pandas as pd
df = pd.read_excel("data.xlsx", sheet_name="Sheet1")
df.to_csv("output.csv", index=False)
```

This converts an Excel sheet to a CSV file.

---

6. How can you clean and transform extracted data automatically?

ANSWER: You can use pandas to handle missing values, normalize text, and remove duplicates:

```
df.drop_duplicates(inplace=True)
df.fillna(method='ffill', inplace=True)
df['column'] = df['column'].str.lower().str.strip()
```

This ensures data quality.

---

7. What is ETL, and how can Python be used for it?

ANSWER: ETL (EXTRACT, Transform, Load) refers to the process of extracting data, transforming it, and loading it into a data warehouse. Python ETL libraries:

- **pandas** (for transformation)
- **SQLAlchemy** (for loading)
- **Airflow** (for scheduling ETL jobs)

---

8. How can you extract and process large datasets efficiently?

ANSWER: Use **chunk processing** with pandas:

```
for chunk in pd.read_csv("large_file.csv", chunksize=10000):
process(chunk)
```

This prevents memory overload.

---

9. How do you extract unstructured data using NLP?

ANSWER: Use **spaCy** or **NLTK:**

```
import spacy
nlp = spacy.load("en_core_web_sm")
doc = nlp("Data analysts extract insights from raw data.")
tokens = [token.text for token in doc]
print(tokens)
```

---

10. How do you connect Python to cloud storage for automated data extraction?

ANSWER: Use **Google Cloud Storage (GCS), AWS S3, or Azure Blob Storage**:

```
from google.cloud import storage
client = storage.Client()
bucket = client.get_bucket('my_bucket')
blob = bucket.blob('data.csv')
blob.download_to_filename('local_data.csv')
```

Section 4: Debugging Common Python Errors in Data Analysis

DEBUGGING IS A CRITICAL skill for data analysts. Below are **common Python errors** encountered in data analysis interviews, along with their solutions.

---

11. What does "KeyError" in pandas mean?

ANSWER: It means the specified key (column or index) is missing. Fix it by checking column names:

```
if 'column_name' in df.columns:
print(df['column_name'])
```

---

12. How do you handle a "ValueError: could not convert string to float"?

ANSWER: Convert data types correctly:

```
df['column'] = pd.to_numeric(df['column'], errors='coerce')
```

---

13. What causes "MemoryError" in pandas, and how do you fix it?

ANSWER: It occurs with large datasets. Solutions:

- Use **dtype optimization**

- Process data in **chunks**
- Use **Dask** instead of pandas

```
import dask.dataframe as dd
df = dd.read_csv("large_file.csv")
```

---

14. What is a "TypeError" and how can you fix it?

ANSWER: It occurs when performing an invalid operation:

```
df['price'] = df['price'].astype(float) # Ensure correct type
```

---

15. How do you fix an "ImportError" in Python?

ANSWER: Ensure the module is installed and imported correctly:

```
pip install pandas
import pandas
```

---

16. How do you handle "ZeroDivisionError"?

ANSWER: Use exception handling:

```
try:
result = 100 / 0
except ZeroDivisionError:
result = None
```

---

17. How do you resolve "AttributeError" in pandas?

ANSWER: Ensure the column exists and is spelled correctly:

```
print(df.columns) # Check column names
```

---

18. What causes a "SyntaxError" in Python?

ANSWER: Syntax mistakes such as missing colons, incorrect indentation, or unmatched parentheses. Example fix:

```
if x == 10: # Missing colon fixed
print(x)
```

---

19. How do you debug a script that runs but gives incorrect

results?

ANSWER: Use **print statements, logging**, or **pdb (Python Debugger)**:

```
import pdb
pdb.set_trace()
```

---

20. How can you handle missing values effectively?

ANSWER: Use pandas methods:

```
df.fillna(value="Unknown", inplace=True)
df.dropna(inplace=True)
```

---

21. What causes a "NameError" in Python?

ANSWER: Using an undefined variable. Solution:

```
x = 10
print(x) # Ensure variable is defined
```

---

22. How do you handle "JSONDecodeError" in Python?

ANSWER: Ensure the JSON format is valid before loading:

```
import json
try:
data = json.loads('{"key": "value"}')
except json.JSONDecodeError:
print("Invalid JSON")
```

Final Thoughts

THIS CHAPTER PROVIDED real-time Python questions and answers for **automating data extraction and debugging common errors.** Mastering these concepts will help you **excel in your data analyst interview** and become **proficient in real-world data analysis tasks.**

Chapter 6: Real-Time Business Case Studies & Problem-Solving

In this chapter, we will walk through real-time business problems that companies face and how data analysts can tackle them effectively. Each section presents a structured approach, covering business context, problem statement, data requirements, analysis techniques, and insights derived from the findings. We will also provide sample interview questions that employers often ask in business case discussions and concise yet impactful responses.

Section 1: Solving a Real Company's Sales Performance Issue

Business Context

A RETAIL COMPANY HAS been experiencing declining sales despite increasing foot traffic in stores. The company wants to understand why revenue is not growing proportionally to the increase in customer visits. As a data analyst, your job is to identify the root cause and provide recommendations.

Problem Statement

THE SALES PERFORMANCE of the company has stagnated, and management needs data-driven insights to determine the cause. Possible reasons could include poor conversion rates, ineffective marketing strategies, pricing issues, or customer dissatisfaction.

Data Required

TO ANALYZE THE PROBLEM, the following datasets are required:

- **Sales Data:** Transaction-level sales, product categories, revenue, and units sold.
- **Customer Data:** Customer demographics, purchase frequency, and average order value.
- **Marketing Data:** Campaign performance, promotional impact, and customer response.
- **Foot Traffic Data:** Number of visitors per store, peak hours, and seasonal trends.
- **Competitor Pricing Data:** Price comparisons with competitors.

Analysis Approach

Step 1: Exploratory Data Analysis (EDA)

- Perform **descriptive statistics** on sales, customer demographics, and product performance.
- Use visualization tools like **histograms, box plots, and scatter plots** to understand sales trends.

Step 2: Identifying Key Sales Metrics

- **Conversion Rate:** Total Transactions/Total Foot Traffic\text{Total Transactions} / \text{Total Foot Traffic}Total Transactions/Total Foot Traffic
- **Average Order Value (AOV):** Total Revenue/Total Orders\text{Total Revenue} / \text{Total Orders}Total Revenue/Total Orders

- **Revenue Per Customer:** Total Revenue/Unique Customers\text{Total Revenue} / \text{Unique Customers}Total Revenue/Unique Customers

Step 3: Identifying Bottlenecks

- Compare sales trends across different stores.

- Analyze conversion rates by region to identify underperforming locations.

- Check if promotions and discounts effectively boost sales.

- Investigate if cart abandonment rates are high due to pricing issues.

Step 4: Competitor & Pricing Analysis

- Compare product pricing with competitors.
- Identify if customers are price-sensitive and switching to competitors.

Step 5: Data-Driven Recommendations

- Improve in-store experience through better product placement and promotions.

- Adjust pricing strategies based on demand elasticity.

- Optimize marketing campaigns based on customer purchasing behavior.

Common Interview Questions & Answers

1. How would you analyze sales performance using data?

ANSWER: I would start by examining historical sales data to identify trends. I'd analyze key metrics like conversion rate, AOV, and revenue per customer. I'd also segment sales by region, product category, and customer demographics to find patterns. Lastly, I would compare our pricing and promotions against competitors.

2. What statistical techniques would you use to identify trends in declining sales?

ANSWER: I would use time series analysis to detect trends and seasonality. Hypothesis testing (such as A/B testing) would help determine if promotions impact sales. Regression analysis can identify factors affecting sales, and clustering techniques can segment customers.

3. If given a dataset with sales transactions, how would you clean and preprocess it?

ANSWER: I would handle missing values, remove duplicates, and standardize formats. I'd also validate data consistency, check for outliers using box plots, and ensure proper data types for numerical and categorical fields.

4. How do you measure the impact of pricing on sales?

ANSWER: I would conduct a price elasticity analysis by measuring how demand changes with different price points. I'd also use A/B testing to compare different pricing strategies and observe customer reactions.

Section 2: Analyzing Churn Rate for a Subscription Business

Business Context

A STREAMING SERVICE provider has observed an increase in customer churn. They want to analyze why subscribers are canceling and what can be done to retain them.

Problem Statement

THE COMPANY NEEDS TO determine the key factors driving churn and develop a strategy to improve customer retention.

Data Required

- **Customer Subscription Data:** Subscription start and end dates, plan types, and payment history.
- **Engagement Data:** Viewing hours, content preferences, and interaction frequency.
- **Support Tickets:** Number of customer complaints, response time, and resolutions.
- **Demographics Data:** Age, location, device usage, and income levels.

Analysis Approach

Step 1: Define Churn Metrics

- **Churn Rate:** Number of Canceled Subscriptions/Total Subscribers\text{Number of Canceled Subscriptions} / \text{Total Subscribers}Number of Canceled Subscriptions/Total Subscribers

- **Average Lifetime Value (LTV):** Average Revenue Per User×Average Subscription Duration\text{Average Revenue Per User} \times \text{Average Subscription Duration}Average Revenue Per User×Average Subscription Duration

- **Engagement Score:** Based on frequency and duration of service usage.

Step 2: Exploratory Data Analysis (EDA)

- Visualize churn trends over time.
- Analyze churn by customer demographics and subscription plans.
- Identify drop-off points where users disengage.

Step 3: Predictive Modeling

- Use **logistic regression** to identify churn probability.
- Apply **decision trees** to segment customers based on risk.
- Use **survival analysis** to estimate the likelihood of long-term retention.

Step 4: Customer Segmentation

- Segment users based on engagement levels (high, medium, low).
- Identify customer profiles that are more likely to churn.

Step 5: Data-Driven Recommendations

- Improve content recommendations using machine learning.
- Offer personalized promotions to high-risk churn customers.
- Enhance customer support and reduce response times.

Common Interview Questions & Answers

1. What data points would you analyze to understand churn?

ANSWER: I'd analyze subscription history, engagement levels, support interactions, and payment patterns. Additionally, I'd look at competitor impact and customer feedback.

2. How would you predict churn?

ANSWER: I'd use logistic regression to estimate churn probability and decision trees to classify high-risk customers. I'd also leverage survival analysis to predict long-term retention.

3. How do you measure customer engagement?

ANSWER: Engagement can be measured through viewing hours, number of logins, frequency of interactions, and average session duration.

4. What strategies can reduce churn?

ANSWER: Providing personalized recommendations, offering loyalty discounts, improving customer support, and engaging users with targeted content can help reduce churn.

Section 3: Revenue Forecasting Using Historical Data

REVENUE FORECASTING is a crucial aspect of business analytics that helps organizations plan for the future, allocate resources, and set realistic financial goals. In this section, we will cover real-time interview questions related to revenue forecasting, including key techniques, challenges, and solutions.

Question 1: What are the key steps involved in revenue forecasting using historical data?

ANSWER:

The key steps involved in revenue forecasting using historical data are:

1. **Data Collection** – Gather historical revenue data, sales figures, and other relevant business metrics.
2. **Data Cleaning** – Remove inconsistencies, missing values, and outliers.
3. **Data Exploration** – Analyze trends, seasonality, and patterns using visualizations and summary statistics.
4. **Feature Selection** – Identify factors influencing revenue, such as marketing spend, customer behavior, and economic conditions.
5. **Model Selection** – Choose an appropriate forecasting model (e.g., ARIMA, exponential smoothing, regression models).
6. **Model Training & Evaluation** – Split data into training and testing sets, train the model, and evaluate its performance using metrics like RMSE or MAPE.
7. **Forecasting & Interpretation** – Generate forecasts and interpret results to provide actionable insights.

Question 2: Which statistical techniques can be used for revenue forecasting?

ANSWER:

Common statistical techniques for revenue forecasting include:

- **Time Series Analysis (ARIMA, SARIMA)** – Used for analyzing past patterns and making future predictions.

- **Regression Analysis** – Determines relationships between independent variables (e.g., ad spend, seasonality) and revenue.

- **Exponential Smoothing (Holt-Winters Method)** – Useful for capturing trends and seasonality in time series data.

- **Machine Learning Models (Random Forest, XGBoost, LSTMs)** – Used for complex forecasting with multiple influencing factors.

Question 3: How would you handle seasonality in revenue forecasting?

ANSWER:

To handle seasonality, we can:

- Use **seasonal decomposition** to separate trend, seasonality, and residual components.

- Apply **SARIMA (Seasonal ARIMA)** to model seasonal patterns explicitly.

- Use **Fourier transforms** or dummy variables in regression models.

- Normalize data using **moving averages** or differencing techniques to remove seasonal effects.

Question 4: What are the key challenges in revenue forecasting, and how do you address them?

ANSWER:

Key challenges include:

- **Data Quality Issues** – Missing, inconsistent, or inaccurate data can lead to poor forecasts. Solution: Clean data and use imputation techniques.

- **Market Fluctuations** – Economic downturns, policy changes, or competitor actions can impact forecasts. Solution: Incorporate external data sources and scenario analysis.

- **Seasonality & Trends** – Fluctuating demand can impact accuracy. Solution: Use models that account for seasonality and trend shifts.

- **Limited Historical Data** – Insufficient data can hinder model performance. Solution: Use transfer learning or alternative data sources.

Question 5: Can you explain the role of external factors in revenue forecasting?

ANSWER:

External factors such as economic conditions, competitor pricing, marketing campaigns, and consumer trends can significantly influence revenue. To incorporate them:

- Use **macroeconomic indicators** (e.g., GDP growth, inflation rates).
- Include **customer sentiment analysis** from social media or surveys.
- Integrate **industry reports** and competitor data for better forecasting.

Question 6: How do you evaluate the accuracy of a revenue forecasting model?

ANSWER:

Common evaluation metrics include:

- **Mean Absolute Percentage Error (MAPE)** – Measures forecast accuracy as a percentage.

- **Root Mean Squared Error (RMSE)** – Penalizes larger errors more heavily.

- **Mean Absolute Error (MAE)** – Averages absolute differences between actual and predicted values.

- **R-squared** – Measures how well the model explains variance in the data.

Section 4: Case Study – Identifying Key Business Trends

IDENTIFYING BUSINESS trends is essential for making data-driven decisions. Companies analyze sales data, customer behavior, and market conditions to stay ahead of the competition. This section presents real-time interview questions on trend analysis and business insights.

Question 7: How would you identify key business trends from sales data?

ANSWER:

To identify trends:

- Perform **time series analysis** to detect patterns.
- Use **moving averages** to smooth fluctuations.
- Apply **clustering techniques** (e.g., K-Means) to segment data.
- Compare **year-over-year (YoY) and month-over-month (MoM) growth** metrics.

Question 8: What tools would you use for trend analysis?

ANSWER:

Common tools include:

- **SQL & Python (Pandas, NumPy, Matplotlib, Seaborn)** for data extraction and visualization.
- **Power BI & Tableau** for interactive dashboards.
- **Google Analytics** for website traffic trends.
- **Time Series Forecasting Libraries (Statsmodels, Scikit-learn, Prophet)** for predictive analysis.

Question 9: Can you give an example of a real-world business trend analysis?

ANSWER:
Example: An **e-commerce company** noticed a **decline in weekend sales.** Analyzing data revealed that competitors offered discounts on weekends. The company launched its own promotional campaigns to regain lost sales.

Question 10: How do you differentiate between a short-term fluctuation and a long-term trend?

ANSWER:

- **Short-term fluctuations** are temporary spikes due to events (e.g., holiday sales).
- **Long-term trends** are consistent patterns over months or years, analyzed using linear regression or moving averages.

Question 11: How do you handle anomalies in trend analysis?

ANSWER:

- Use **Z-score or IQR methods** to detect outliers.
- Apply **smoothing techniques** (e.g., rolling averages).
- Investigate anomalies manually before removing or adjusting data.

Question 12: What are leading vs. lagging indicators in trend analysis?

ANSWER:

- **Leading Indicators** – Predict future trends (e.g., website traffic, customer inquiries).

- **Lagging Indicators** – Confirm past trends (e.g., sales revenue, profit margins).

Question 13: How would you present key business trends to stakeholders?

ANSWER:
Use:

- **Data visualizations** (e.g., line charts, bar graphs).
- **Comparative reports** showing past vs. current performance.
- **Storytelling with data** to make insights actionable.

Question 14: What challenges arise in business trend identification?

ANSWER:

- **Data inconsistency** – Solution: Use data validation techniques.
- **Market disruptions** – Solution: Adjust models dynamically.
- **Overfitting in models** – Solution: Use cross-validation.

Question 15: What is an example of a company successfully identifying a

trend early?

ANSWER:

Example: **Netflix** identified a trend in streaming and shifted focus from DVD rentals to digital content, gaining a competitive advantage.

Revenue forecasting and trend analysis are essential for business decision-making. Strong data analysis skills, statistical techniques, and effective communication help analysts extract meaningful insights and drive business success. Mastering these real-world scenarios will prepare you for a data analyst interview with confidence.

Chapter 7: Statistics & A/B Testing in Real-Life Interviews

Section 1: Applying Statistical Concepts to Business Decisions

1. What is the Central Limit Theorem (CLT), and why is it important in business decision-making?

Answer:

The Central Limit Theorem states that the distribution of the sample mean approaches a normal distribution as the sample size increases, regardless of the population's distribution. This is crucial in business because it allows analysts to make predictions and inferences using normal distribution properties, enabling more accurate forecasting, hypothesis testing, and confidence interval estimation.

2. How do you determine whether to use mean vs. median in analyzing business data?

ANSWER:

Use **mean** when the data is normally distributed and free from extreme values. Use **median** when the data has outliers or is skewed, as the median is less affected by extreme values and provides a better measure of central tendency.

3. What is p-value, and how is it used in statistical decision-making?

ANSWER:

A p-value represents the probability of obtaining test results as extreme as the observed results under the null hypothesis. If **p-value ≤ 0.05**, we reject the null hypothesis, suggesting strong evidence against it. If **p-value > 0.05**, we fail to reject the null hypothesis, meaning there is not enough evidence to prove an effect.

4. Explain Type I and Type II errors with an example in a business scenario.

ANSWER:

- **Type I Error (False Positive):** Rejecting a true null hypothesis. Example: A bank falsely detects fraud in a non-fraudulent transaction.

- **Type II Error (False Negative):** Failing to reject a false null hypothesis. Example: A marketing campaign is successful, but the test fails to detect its impact, leading the company to abandon it.

5. What is standard deviation, and why is it important in business analytics?

ANSWER:

Standard deviation measures the dispersion of data points from the mean. A **low standard deviation** indicates that data points are close to the mean (consistent performance), whereas a **high standard deviation** suggests more variability (unstable performance). Businesses use it to measure risk in investments, customer satisfaction variation, and sales performance fluctuations.

6. How do you determine if a dataset is normally distributed?

ANSWER:

- **Visual Inspection:** Histogram or Q-Q plot

- **Statistical Tests:** Shapiro-Wilk test, Kolmogorov-Smirnov test

- **Skewness & Kurtosis:** Skewness near 0 and kurtosis near 3 suggest normality

- **Empirical Rule:** In a normal distribution, ~68% of data falls within 1 SD, ~95% within 2 SD, and ~99.7% within 3 SD.

7. What is the difference between correlation and causation?

ANSWER:

Correlation means two variables move together but do not necessarily influence each other. **Causation** means one variable directly affects another. Example: Ice cream sales and drowning deaths are correlated (both increase in summer) but do not cause each other.

8. What is multicollinearity, and why is it a problem in regression analysis?

ANSWER:

Multicollinearity occurs when independent variables in a regression model are highly correlated, making it difficult to determine the impact of each variable. It can be detected using **Variance Inflation Factor (VIF)**, and resolved by **removing correlated variables** or using **principal component analysis (PCA)**.

9. What is the difference between a t-test and a chi-square test?

ANSWER:

- **T-test** compares **means** of two groups (e.g., comparing sales in two regions).

- **Chi-square test** examines **categorical data** for independence (e.g., whether product preference is related to gender).

10. How would you handle missing data in a dataset?

ANSWER:

- **Remove** rows/columns with excessive missing values
- **Impute** using mean, median, or mode
- **Use predictive models** (KNN, regression) to estimate missing values
- **Flag missing values** and analyze patterns

Section 2: Conducting A/B Tests for Product Optimization

11. What is an A/B test, and why is it used?

ANSWER:

A/B testing compares two versions of a product or feature to determine which performs better based on key metrics. It is used in website design, marketing campaigns, and product improvements to **data-driven decision-making.**

12. What are the key components of an A/B test?

ANSWER:

- **Control Group (A):** Baseline version
- **Treatment Group (B):** Modified version
- **Randomization:** Ensures fair comparison
- **Key Metrics:** Click-through rate (CTR), conversion rate, revenue per user
- **Significance Testing:** Ensures differences are not due to chance

13. How do you decide the sample size for an A/B test?

ANSWER:

Use **power analysis** to determine sample size based on:

- **Effect Size:** Expected impact of the change
- **Significance Level (α):** Usually 0.05

- **Power (1-β):** Typically 0.8, meaning an 80% chance of detecting an effect

14. What are some common pitfalls in A/B testing?

ANSWER:

- **Running tests too short** (risk of false positives)
- **Stopping tests early** (inconclusive results)
- **Multiple comparisons** (increases Type I errors)
- **Biased randomization** (unequal groups)

15. What is the difference between one-tailed and two-tailed tests in A/B testing?

ANSWER:

- **One-tailed test:** Tests for an effect in **one** direction (e.g., new version is better).

- **Two-tailed test:** Tests for an effect in **both** directions (e.g., new version could be better or worse).

16. What metrics should be considered when evaluating an A/B test?

ANSWER:

- **Conversion Rate:** Percentage of users completing desired action
- **Revenue Per User:** Measures revenue impact
- **Bounce Rate:** Tracks user engagement
- **Retention Rate:** Determines long-term impact

17. How do you handle statistical significance vs. practical significance in A/B tests?

ANSWER:

A statistically significant result ($p < 0.05$) may not be practically useful if the effect size is small. Businesses must balance **statistical evidence** with **real-world impact.**

18. How would you interpret an A/B test where the difference is not statistically significant?

ANSWER:

- **Check power and sample size**
- **Consider business impact despite p-value**
- **Analyze secondary metrics**
- **Run a longer test if needed**

19. How do you avoid peeking bias in A/B testing?

ANSWER:

Peeking bias occurs when results are checked before the test is complete, increasing false positives. Solutions:

- Set a fixed test duration
- Use sequential testing methods

20. Can you run more than two variations in an A/B test?

ANSWER:

Yes, this is called an **A/B/n test**, but it requires larger sample sizes to detect meaningful differences among multiple versions.

Section 3: Real-World Hypothesis Testing Scenarios

HYPOTHESIS TESTING is a fundamental concept in statistics, frequently tested in data analyst interviews. Employers expect candidates to demonstrate their ability to design, conduct, and interpret hypothesis tests in real-world business scenarios. The following interview questions and answers will help you prepare effectively.

---

1. What is hypothesis testing, and why is it important in data analysis?

ANSWER: Hypothesis testing is a statistical method used to make inferences about a population based on sample data. It helps businesses validate assumptions and make data-driven decisions by determining whether observed differences or relationships are statistically significant.

---

2. Explain the null hypothesis (H_0) and the alternative hypothesis (H_1).

ANSWER:

- **Null Hypothesis (H_0):** Assumes there is no effect or difference in the population (e.g., a new marketing strategy does not increase sales).
- **Alternative Hypothesis (H_1):** Suggests there is an effect or difference (e.g., the new marketing strategy leads to increased sales).

---

3. How do you decide whether to reject the null hypothesis?

ANSWER: We compare the p-value of the test with a predefined significance level (α, usually 0.05). If the p-value is less than α, we reject H_0, indicating strong evidence in favor of H_1.

---

4. What are Type I and Type II errors? How do they impact decision-making?

ANSWER:

- **Type I Error (False Positive):** Rejecting H_0 when it is actually true (e.g., concluding a new drug works when it doesn't).
- **Type II Error (False Negative):** Failing to reject H_0 when H_1 is true (e.g., missing a successful new marketing campaign).

Balancing these errors is crucial for making reliable business decisions.

---

5. Can you explain p-value in simple terms?

ANSWER: The p-value represents the probability of obtaining the observed results (or more extreme ones) if H_0 is true. A small p-value (<0.05) suggests strong evidence against H_0, while a large p-value suggests insufficient evidence to reject H_0.

---

6. What is the difference between a one-tailed and a two-tailed test?

ANSWER:

- **One-tailed test:** Checks for an effect in one specific direction (e.g., whether a new ad campaign increases sales).
- **Two-tailed test:** Tests for an effect in both directions (e.g., whether a new drug has either a positive or negative effect).

---

7. When should you use a t-test vs. a z-test?

ANSWER:

- **Z-test:** Used when the population standard deviation is known and the sample size is large ($n > 30$).
- **T-test:** Used when the population standard deviation is unknown and the sample size is small ($n \leq 30$).

---

8. What is an A/B test, and how does it relate to hypothesis testing?

ANSWER: A/B testing is a controlled experiment comparing two variations (A and B) to determine which performs better. It is a practical application of hypothesis testing where H_0 assumes no difference between A and B, while H_1 suggests one is superior.

9. How do you determine the sample size for an A/B test?

ANSWER: The sample size depends on the desired statistical power (typically 80%), significance level ($\alpha = 0.05$), and the expected effect size. Tools like power analysis can help determine the optimal sample size.

10. What is statistical power, and why is it important?

ANSWER: Statistical power ($1 - \beta$) is the probability of correctly rejecting H_0 when H_1 is true. High power reduces the risk of Type II errors, ensuring the test can detect meaningful differences.

Section 4: Case Study – Improving Conversion Rates Using Statistics

Scenario: Optimizing an E-commerce Checkout Process

A LEADING E-COMMERCE company notices a high cart abandonment rate. To improve conversions, they test a new one-click checkout system (Version B) against the existing multi-step checkout (Version A).

11. How would you set up the hypothesis test for this A/B experiment?

ANSWER:

- **H_0:** The conversion rate of the new checkout system (B) is the same as the old one (A).
- **H_1:** The new checkout system (B) has a higher conversion rate than the old one (A).

12. What type of statistical test would you use?

ANSWER: A two-sample proportion z-test is appropriate since we are comparing conversion rates (proportions) between two independent groups (A and B).

---

13. How do you ensure the test results are statistically significant?

ANSWER: We ensure statistical significance by:

- Choosing an appropriate sample size.
- Using a 95% confidence level ($\alpha = 0.05$).
- Ensuring a p-value < 0.05 to reject H_0.

---

14. What role does the confidence interval play in A/B testing?

ANSWER: The confidence interval estimates the range within which the true difference in conversion rates lies. If the confidence interval does not contain zero, it indicates a significant difference.

---

15. What if the p-value is slightly above 0.05? Should we still consider the result?

ANSWER: If the p-value is close to 0.05, it suggests borderline significance. We may increase the sample size or conduct further analysis before making a business decision.

---

16. How do you account for seasonality in A/B testing?

ANSWER: We run the test long enough to capture variations across different days and times. Additionally, we can segment results by time periods to ensure no bias due to seasonality.

---

17. What is a practical significance vs. statistical significance?

ANSWER:

- **Statistical Significance:** Determined by p-values and confidence intervals.
- **Practical Significance:** Assesses whether the detected effect size is meaningful for business decisions.

---

18. How can A/A testing help improve A/B test reliability?

ANSWER: A/A testing (comparing identical groups) helps verify the test setup, ensuring there is no hidden bias or uneven distribution before running an actual A/B test.

---

19. What happens if one variation wins early in an A/B test?

ANSWER: Premature conclusions can be misleading. It's best to run the test until reaching the required sample size for statistical validity.

---

20. How do you deal with peeking in A/B testing?

ANSWER: Peeking (checking results too frequently) inflates Type I errors. To avoid this, we predefine the sample size and only analyze results once the test is complete.

---

21. How do you handle multiple A/B tests running simultaneously?

ANSWER: We use Bonferroni correction or false discovery rate control to adjust for multiple comparisons, ensuring valid results.

---

22. How do you interpret a statistically significant result in an A/B test?

ANSWER: A statistically significant result means there's strong evidence against H_0. However, we must also check the effect size to determine practical significance.

---

23. What are some common pitfalls in A/B testing?

ANSWER:

- Running the test for too short a duration.
- Not accounting for seasonality.
- Peeking at results prematurely.
- Ignoring the practical significance of findings.

---

24. How do you present A/B test results to non-technical stakeholders?

ANSWER:

- Use visualizations (bar charts, line graphs).
- Explain findings in simple terms.
- Highlight business impact, not just statistical details.

A strong understanding of hypothesis testing and A/B testing is essential for data analysts. Mastering these concepts will help you excel in real-life interviews and make data-driven business decisions.

Chapter 8: Excel Power Tricks & Real-World Scenarios

Section 1: Advanced Formulas (VLOOKUP, INDEX-MATCH, Pivot Tables)

Q1: What is VLOOKUP, and how does it work?

Answer:

VLOOKUP (Vertical Lookup) is a function in Excel used to search for a value in the first column of a range and return a value from a specified column in the same row. Its syntax is:

VLOOKUP(lookup_value, table_array, col_index_num, [range_lookup])

- lookup_value: The value to search for.
- table_array: The table where the search is performed.
- col_index_num: The column number from which the value should be returned.
- range_lookup: TRUE (approximate match) or FALSE (exact match).

Example: If we want to find an employee's salary from a table using their employee ID, we can use:

=VLOOKUP(1001, A2:D10, 3, FALSE)

This finds employee ID "1001" in column A and returns the value from the 3rd column.

Q2: What are the limitations of VLOOKUP?

ANSWER:

- It only searches in the first column of the range.
- It cannot look to the left of the lookup column.
- It is slower for large datasets compared to INDEX-MATCH.
- It requires an exact column index, making maintenance harder.

Q3: What is INDEX-MATCH, and why is it better than VLOOKUP?

ANSWER:

INDEX-MATCH is a powerful alternative to VLOOKUP. It combines the INDEX function (which returns a value from a specified row and column) with MATCH (which finds the position of a value in a column or row).

Syntax:

=INDEX(array, MATCH(lookup_value, lookup_array, match_type))

Example: To find an employee's salary when the Employee ID is in column A and salary in column D:

=INDEX(D2:D10, MATCH(1001, A2:A10, 0))

Advantages over VLOOKUP:

- Can look up values in any direction (not just to the right).
- Faster for large datasets.
- More flexible and less prone to breaking when columns are inserted or deleted.

Q4: When should you use Pivot Tables in Excel?

ANSWER:

Pivot Tables are best for summarizing, analyzing, and extracting insights from large datasets. Use them when:

- You need to calculate sums, averages, or counts dynamically.
- You want to group data by categories or time periods.
- You need to generate reports without modifying the raw data.

Q5: How do you create a Pivot Table?

ANSWER:

1. Select the dataset.
2. Go to **Insert > Pivot Table.**
3. Choose where to place the Pivot Table (New or Existing Worksheet).
4. Drag fields into **Rows, Columns, Values, and Filters** sections as needed.
5. Customize using **Value Field Settings** (sum, count, average, etc.).

Q6: How do you use Slicers in Pivot Tables?

ANSWER:

Slicers provide an interactive way to filter Pivot Tables. To add a Slicer:

1. Click anywhere on the Pivot Table.
2. Go to **Insert > Slicer.**
3. Select the fields you want as filters.
4. Click on a Slicer button to filter data instantly.

Q7: How do you refresh Pivot Tables automatically?

ANSWER:

To ensure the Pivot Table updates when the dataset changes:

- Right-click on the Pivot Table and select **Refresh**.
- Use VBA to auto-refresh:

```
Private Sub Worksheet_Change(ByVal Target As Range)
```

```
Sheets("Sheet1").PivotTables("PivotTable1").PivotCache.Refresh
End Sub
```

Section 2: Automating Reports with Macros

Q8: What is a Macro in Excel?

ANSWER:

A Macro is a recorded set of actions in Excel that automates repetitive tasks. Macros use VBA (Visual Basic for Applications) to execute commands automatically.

Q9: How do you record a Macro in Excel?

ANSWER:

1. Go to **Developer** tab (enable it from Excel options if hidden).
2. Click **Record Macro**.
3. Provide a name and optional shortcut key.
4. Perform the actions you want to automate.
5. Click **Stop Recording** to finish.

Q10: How do you run a Macro?

ANSWER:

- Use the shortcut key assigned.
- Click **Developer** > **Macros** > Select the Macro > Click **Run**.
- Use a button (Insert a shape, right-click, assign Macro).

Q11: What are some real-world applications of Macros?

ANSWER:

- Automating data cleaning.
- Creating custom reports.

- Sending automated emails from Excel.
- Bulk updating and formatting data.

Q12: How do you write a simple VBA Macro?

ANSWER:

Example: A Macro to autofill column A based on the last row:

```
Sub AutoFillColumnA()
Dim lastRow As Long
lastRow = Cells(Rows.Count, 1).End(xlUp).Row
Range("A2:A" & lastRow).Formula = "=B2+C2"
End Sub
```

Q13: How can you debug a Macro in VBA?

ANSWER:

- Use **Step Into (F8)** to execute line-by-line.
- Add **MsgBox** statements to check values.
- Use **Breakpoints** to pause code execution.
- Check the **Immediate Window** for quick testing.

Q14: What are the risks of using Macros?

ANSWER:

- Security risks (Macros can contain harmful code).
- Can become slow for large data.
- Errors in code can break automation.

Q15: How do you protect your Macros from unauthorized access?

ANSWER:

- Lock VBA with a password (**Developer** > **Visual Basic** > **Tools** > **VBAProject Properties** > **Lock Project for Viewing**).

- Save the file as **.xlsm** format.

Q16: How do you create a Macro that runs automatically when opening a workbook?

ANSWER:

Place the code inside the Workbook_Open event in **ThisWorkbook** module:

```
Private Sub Workbook_Open()
MsgBox "Welcome to the Report!"
End Sub
```

Q17: How do you loop through rows in VBA?

ANSWER:

```
Sub LoopThroughRows()
Dim i As Integer
For i = 2 To 100
Cells(i, 3).Value = Cells(i, 1).Value + Cells(i, 2).Value
Next i
End Sub
```

Q18: How do you send emails from Excel using VBA?

ANSWER:

```
Sub SendEmail()
Dim OutlookApp As Object
Dim MailItem As Object
Set OutlookApp = CreateObject("Outlook.Application")
Set MailItem = OutlookApp.CreateItem(0)
With MailItem
.To = "email@example.com"
.Subject = "Automated Report"
```

```
.Body = "Please find the report attached."
.Send
End With
End Sub
```

Section 3: Case Study – Creating a Dynamic Sales Report

IN MANY DATA ANALYST interviews, candidates are asked to demonstrate their ability to create insightful and dynamic reports in Excel. The interviewer wants to assess proficiency in formulas, PivotTables, data visualization, and automation techniques. Below is a real-world case study with commonly asked questions and expert answers.

Case Study Background

A RETAIL COMPANY WANTS to track its monthly sales performance dynamically. You have been given a dataset containing sales transactions with the following fields:

- **Date** (Transaction Date)
- **Region** (North, South, East, West)
- **Product Category** (Electronics, Clothing, Furniture, etc.)
- **Salesperson** (Name of the salesperson)
- **Revenue** (Total revenue from the transaction)
- **Units Sold** (Number of units sold)

The goal is to create an interactive dashboard that allows management to analyze sales trends and performance at different levels dynamically.

Interview Questions & Answers

1. How would you structure the dataset for easy analysis?

ANSWER: I would ensure that the dataset is in a tabular format with clearly labeled column headers. Each row should represent a unique transaction, and there should be no merged cells or blank rows. I would also format the data as an Excel Table (Ctrl + T) to enable structured referencing and dynamic range selection in formulas.

2. What Excel functions would you use to clean the dataset before creating the report?

ANSWER: I would use:

- **TRIM()** to remove extra spaces in text fields.
- **CLEAN()** to remove non-printable characters.
- **TEXT()** to format dates correctly.
- **IFERROR()** to handle missing or incorrect values.

3. How would you handle missing or incorrect data in the dataset?

ANSWER: I would use the **COUNTBLANK()** function to identify missing values and then:

- Use **IF()** statements to replace missing values with a default or calculated value.

- Remove rows with excessive missing data if appropriate.

- Use **Find & Replace** or **Power Query** to fix incorrect entries.

4. How would you create a summary report of total revenue and units sold by region?

ANSWER: I would use a **PivotTable**, placing "Region" in the **Rows** section and "Revenue" and "Units Sold" in the **Values** section. I would set the value field settings to **Sum** to get total revenue and units sold per region.

5. How can you make the report dynamic so that users can filter sales data by product category or salesperson?

ANSWER: I would insert a **Slicer** for the "Product Category" and "Salesperson" fields. Slicers provide an interactive way to filter data within the PivotTable and update the report dynamically.

6. How would you create a revenue trend analysis over time?

ANSWER: I would use a **PivotTable with a Date field** in the Rows section and group it by **Month and Year**. Then, I would insert a **Pivot Chart (Line Chart)** to visualize revenue trends over time.

7. How can you highlight salespeople who have exceeded a certain revenue target?

ANSWER: I would use **Conditional Formatting** with a formula like:
=B2>50000 (if column B contains revenue) and apply formatting like bold text or color highlights to emphasize top performers.

8. How would you automate data refresh if the dataset is updated frequently?

ANSWER: I would connect the dataset to **Power Query**, load it into the workbook, and set the query to refresh automatically when the file opens.

9. How would you compare this year's sales with the previous year?

ANSWER: I would create a **Year-over-Year (YoY) growth analysis** using the **GETPIVOTDATA()** function or **DAX formulas in Power Pivot** to calculate percentage change.

10. How would you create a drop-down menu to filter data dynamically?

ANSWER: I would use **Data Validation** to create a drop-down list and use **INDEX-MATCH()** or **XLOOKUP()** to dynamically display filtered data based on user selection.

Section 4: Handling Large Datasets in Excel Efficiently

WHEN DEALING WITH LARGE datasets, performance issues can arise. The following questions and answers focus on optimizing Excel for handling large amounts of data efficiently.

Interview Questions & Answers

11. How would you handle datasets with over 1 million rows in Excel?

ANSWER: Since Excel has a row limit of 1,048,576, I would:

- Use **Power Query** to load and transform data.
- Use **Power Pivot** to perform calculations on large datasets.
- Store data in an external database (e.g., SQL) and connect via **Power Query** for analysis.

12. What Excel features help improve performance with large datasets?

ANSWER: Key features include:

- **Power Query** for efficient data transformation.
- **Power Pivot** for handling large datasets with efficient DAX calculations.
- **PivotTables** instead of formulas for summary calculations.
- **Tables instead of named ranges** for structured referencing.

13. How do you prevent Excel from slowing down when working with large files?

ANSWER:

- Avoid **volatile formulas** like OFFSET() and INDIRECT().
- Reduce the number of **array formulas.**
- Use **manual calculation mode** (Formulas → Calculation Options → Manual).
- Optimize formatting and remove unnecessary conditional formatting.

14. What is the difference between a normal PivotTable and Power Pivot?

ANSWER:

- **PivotTables** work with in-memory data but are limited to 1,048,576 rows.

- **Power Pivot** uses the VertiPaq engine, which compresses data efficiently and allows advanced DAX calculations.

15. How can you join multiple datasets in Excel efficiently?

ANSWER: Use **Power Query Merge** to combine datasets based on a common key, avoiding inefficient **VLOOKUP()** formulas.

16. What is the advantage of using Power Query for cleaning large datasets?

ANSWER: Power Query allows for repeatable and automated data cleaning without modifying the original dataset, improving efficiency and accuracy.

17. How do you remove duplicates efficiently in large datasets?

ANSWER: Use **Remove Duplicates** in Power Query instead of the standard Excel feature for better performance.

18. How would you analyze customer sales trends in a dataset with millions of records?

ANSWER: I would load data into **Power Pivot**, create a **Date Table**, and use **DAX measures** to analyze trends efficiently.

19. How can you extract specific insights from large text datasets in Excel?

ANSWER: Use:

- **Text-to-Columns** for splitting data.
- **Power Query transformations** for cleaning.
- **SEARCH(), MID(), and LEFT() functions** for extracting specific information.

20. How do you optimize PivotTables for large datasets?

ANSWER:

- Use **Power Pivot** instead of standard PivotTables.
- Keep source data formatted as a Table.
- Use efficient aggregation instead of complex calculated fields.

21. What is the best way to store large datasets in Excel?

ANSWER: Convert data to a **binary format (.xlsb)** to reduce file size and improve performance.

22. How would you compare two large datasets for differences?

ANSWER: Use **Power Query Merge** or **COUNTIF()** to identify unmatched records efficiently.

23. How can you dynamically filter large datasets in Excel?

ANSWER: Use **Slicers and Timelines** with PivotTables or Power Pivot to allow interactive filtering.

24. What Excel tools are best for working with external databases?

ANSWER: POWER QUERY, Power Pivot, and ODBC connections allow seamless integration with databases like SQL Server.

25. How can you visualize large datasets effectively in Excel?

ANSWER: Use **PivotCharts, Conditional Formatting, and Data Bars** to highlight key trends.

This chapter provides practical, real-world Excel techniques to help candidates demonstrate their skills effectively in data analyst interviews. The ability to manage and analyze large datasets dynamically is crucial in today's data-driven world.

Chapter 9: Behavioral Interview Questions for Data Analysts

Landing a data analyst role requires more than just technical expertise. Employers also assess candidates on their problem-solving skills, communication, adaptability, and how well they fit within the company culture. Behavioral interview questions help hiring managers evaluate these qualities.

This chapter covers **behavioral interview questions** asked in data analyst interviews, along with short yet structured answers. You will also learn the **STAR method (Situation, Task, Action, Result)** to craft impactful responses.

Section 1: Common HR and Situational Questions

1. Tell me about yourself.

ANSWER:

I have been working as a data analyst for [X years] with expertise in SQL, Python, and data visualization tools like Tableau and Power BI. In my current role at [Company Name], I analyze business trends, create reports, and provide insights that drive strategic decisions. I am particularly passionate about using data to solve complex problems and improve business performance.

2. Why do you want to work for our company?

ANSWER:

I am excited about this opportunity because your company emphasizes data-driven decision-making. I admire [Company Name]'s innovation in [Industry], and I believe my experience in data analysis aligns with your needs.

The role also presents a great opportunity to work with a talented team and contribute meaningfully.

3. What are your strengths as a data analyst?

ANSWER:

One of my key strengths is my analytical mindset—I excel at breaking down complex datasets to uncover meaningful insights. Additionally, I have strong SQL and Python skills, allowing me to manipulate data efficiently. My ability to communicate findings in a clear and actionable way also sets me apart.

4. What is your biggest weakness?

ANSWER:

Early in my career, I focused too much on technical accuracy and sometimes struggled to simplify insights for non-technical stakeholders. However, I have worked on improving my storytelling skills by tailoring my presentations to my audience and focusing on the key business impact.

5. Describe a time when you had to explain technical concepts to a non-technical audience.

ANSWER:

At [Company Name], I worked on a project analyzing customer churn. After finding key trends, I presented my findings to the marketing team. Instead of using technical jargon, I focused on visual storytelling with simple charts and real-world examples. As a result, the team was able to adjust their strategy and reduce churn by 15%.

6. Have you ever dealt with a difficult stakeholder? How did you handle it?

ANSWER:

Yes, I once worked with a stakeholder who frequently changed data requirements. To address this, I set up a structured meeting to clarify expectations and aligned on key deliverables. This proactive communication reduced confusion and improved the project's efficiency.

7. Can you tell me about a time when you made a mistake and how you handled it?

ANSWER:

In an analysis report, I overlooked a data discrepancy, which led to an incorrect revenue forecast. Upon realizing the error, I immediately informed my manager, corrected the data, and revised the report. I also implemented a double-checking process to prevent similar issues in the future.

8. How do you handle tight deadlines?

ANSWER:

I prioritize tasks using a structured approach. For example, in a past role, I had to deliver a report within 24 hours. I first identified key priorities, automated repetitive tasks using Python, and worked in collaboration with colleagues. This helped me meet the deadline while maintaining accuracy.

9. Tell me about a time you worked on a team project.

ANSWER:

In my last role, I collaborated with a cross-functional team on a customer segmentation project. My role was to analyze purchase behavior using SQL and Tableau. By working closely with marketing and product teams, we developed data-driven customer profiles that improved targeting and increased conversions.

10. How do you ensure data accuracy in your analysis?

ANSWER:

I always validate data sources, clean datasets thoroughly, and perform sanity checks before drawing conclusions. Additionally, I use version control and peer reviews to ensure accuracy before sharing insights.

Section 2: Answering with the STAR Method

11. Give an example of how you improved a process using data.

ANSWER (STAR METHOD):

- **Situation:** In my previous role, report generation took excessive time due to manual data extraction.
- **Task:** My goal was to automate this process to improve efficiency.
- **Action:** I developed a Python script that automated data extraction and scheduled reports using SQL queries.
- **Result:** This reduced reporting time by 60% and allowed teams to make faster decisions.

12. Describe a time you handled conflicting priorities.

ANSWER (STAR METHOD):

- **Situation:** I was working on two critical projects with overlapping deadlines.
- **Task:** I needed to prioritize tasks without compromising quality.
- **Action:** I assessed the urgency, discussed expectations with stakeholders, and delegated minor tasks.
- **Result:** I successfully delivered both projects on time without errors.

13. Tell me about a time you analyzed a large dataset to solve a problem.

ANSWER (STAR METHOD):

- **Situation:** The company wanted to understand customer churn patterns.
- **Task:** My objective was to identify key factors influencing churn.
- **Action:** I used SQL to extract customer data, performed exploratory analysis in Python, and built a predictive model.
- **Result:** My analysis revealed pricing as a major factor, leading to adjustments that reduced churn by 10%.

14. Give an example of when you had to learn a new tool quickly.

ANSWER (STAR METHOD):

- **Situation:** My team transitioned from Excel to Power BI for reporting.
- **Task:** I needed to upskill myself quickly to maintain reporting efficiency.
- **Action:** I completed an online Power BI course and practiced with real datasets.
- **Result:** Within a month, I created automated dashboards that enhanced data visualization.

15. Describe a time you provided a business recommendation using data.

ANSWER (STAR METHOD):

- **Situation:** Sales were declining in a specific region.
- **Task:** I needed to uncover the root cause and suggest solutions.

- **Action:** I analyzed transaction data and customer demographics, revealing a shift in buying behavior.
- **Result:** My recommendations led to targeted marketing strategies, boosting sales by 12%.

16. Tell me about a time you successfully influenced a business decision.

ANSWER (STAR METHOD):

- **Situation:** The company was planning to expand a product line.
- **Task:** My role was to analyze market trends and customer preferences.
- **Action:** I performed data analysis and presented insights showing higher demand for a different product variant.
- **Result:** The company adjusted its strategy, leading to a more successful product launch.

17. Have you ever handled a dataset with missing or inconsistent data?

ANSWER (STAR METHOD):

- **Situation:** A sales dataset contained missing values and duplicate entries.
- **Task:** I needed to clean and standardize the data for accurate analysis.
- **Action:** I used Python (Pandas) for data imputation and SQL for deduplication.
- **Result:** The cleaned data improved reporting accuracy and prevented faulty insights.

Section 3: Real-World Examples from Top Tech Interviews

BEHAVIORAL INTERVIEWS play a crucial role in the hiring process for data analysts. Top tech companies like Google, Amazon, Microsoft, and Facebook often ask scenario-based questions to evaluate problem-solving skills, communication, and business acumen. Below are real-time questions from these interviews, along with expert short answers.

1. Tell me about a time when you used data to solve a business problem.

ANSWER:

At my previous company, website traffic was declining, and management was unsure why. I analyzed web analytics and discovered that a significant number of users dropped off at the checkout page. Further analysis showed that a recent update increased load time, discouraging purchases. I presented my findings to the engineering team, who optimized the page, leading to a 15% increase in conversions.

2. Can you describe a time when you had to explain a complex analysis to a non-technical stakeholder?

ANSWER:

In a sales performance review, I had to explain why a particular region underperformed. Instead of using complex statistical terms, I used simple charts to show trends in sales, customer engagement, and product demand. I linked the issue to a competitor's aggressive pricing strategy and suggested promotional campaigns, which helped leadership make an informed decision.

3. Describe a time when you had conflicting priorities. How did you handle it?

ANSWER:

I was tasked with preparing a monthly sales report while also working on an urgent ad-hoc analysis for leadership. I communicated the conflicting priorities with my manager and stakeholders, set expectations, and prioritized the ad-hoc request while automating parts of the sales report. This allowed me to complete both tasks efficiently.

4. Tell me about a situation where you faced resistance while implementing a data-driven recommendation.

ANSWER:

I recommended shifting marketing spend from social media ads to email campaigns based on data insights. The marketing team was skeptical, so I ran a small A/B test that showed a 20% higher ROI for email campaigns. The results convinced them to gradually adjust their strategy, leading to improved conversion rates.

5. Have you ever made a mistake in your analysis? How did you handle it?

ANSWER:

Yes, I once overlooked a data pipeline error that led to incorrect revenue forecasting. After identifying the mistake, I immediately informed my manager, corrected the analysis, and implemented additional data validation checks to prevent future errors.

6. How do you prioritize multiple requests from different stakeholders?

ANSWER:

I evaluate each request based on business impact, urgency, and dependencies. I communicate with stakeholders to align on priorities and negotiate deadlines when necessary. If needed, I involve my manager to help resolve conflicts.

7. Describe a time when you used data to drive a strategic decision.

ANSWER:

I conducted an analysis that showed customers with a certain purchase behavior were 40% more likely to subscribe to a premium service. I presented this insight to the marketing team, who then launched targeted promotions, increasing premium subscriptions by 12%.

8. Have you ever dealt with messy or incomplete data? How did you handle it?

ANSWER:

Yes, in a customer retention analysis, I found that purchase history data was incomplete for some users. I collaborated with the engineering team to improve data collection processes and used statistical imputation techniques to fill missing values for the analysis.

9. Describe a time when you had to influence a decision using data.

ANSWER:

I identified that a company's churn rate was highest among users who didn't engage within the first week. I recommended a personalized onboarding email campaign. A pilot test showed a 15% reduction in churn, leading to its company-wide implementation.

10. How do you ensure the accuracy of your analysis?

ANSWER:

I follow a structured validation process, including data cleaning, cross-checking numbers against known benchmarks, and peer review. I also build sanity checks into my queries to flag anomalies.

11. Have you ever disagreed with a team member on a data-driven decision?

ANSWER:

Yes, a colleague and I had different views on whether to exclude outliers in an analysis. I suggested testing both scenarios and presenting the results to stakeholders, allowing data to guide the final decision.

12. Can you share an example of a time you worked on a cross-functional team?

ANSWER:

I worked with marketing, engineering, and product teams to analyze customer feedback and usage data. Our insights helped prioritize feature updates, leading to a 10% increase in user engagement.

---

13. How do you handle tight deadlines?

ANSWER:

I break tasks into smaller parts, focus on the most critical aspects first, and automate repetitive work. I also communicate proactively if a deadline is at risk.

---

14. Tell me about a time you had to troubleshoot a data issue.

ANSWER:

I noticed a sudden drop in traffic for a product page. I traced the issue to an error in UTM tagging, which was affecting attribution. After fixing the tags, the data flow normalized.

---

15. Have you ever had to clean and preprocess a large dataset?

ANSWER:

Yes, in a customer segmentation project, I handled a dataset with millions of records, dealing with duplicates, missing values, and inconsistent formats. I used Python's Pandas library to automate cleaning, saving significant time.

Section 4: Case Study – Explaining a Complex Data Problem to a Non-Technical Manager

Scenario:

A COMPANY'S CEO NOTICES declining customer retention and asks you, the data analyst, to investigate. After analyzing the data, you find that customers with delayed shipping are more likely to churn.

Approach to Explanation:

1. **Understand the Audience:**
   The CEO may not be familiar with statistical terms, so simplify the explanation without losing key insights.
2. **Use a Narrative:**
   "We analyzed customer behavior and noticed a pattern—customers experiencing shipping delays are leaving at a much higher rate than those who receive orders on time."
3. **Visualize the Problem:**
   Present a simple bar chart comparing churn rates between on-time and delayed deliveries.
4. **Highlight the Business Impact:**
   "We estimate that reducing shipping delays could increase retention by 10%, which translates to an additional $2M in revenue annually."
5. **Offer a Data-Driven Solution:**
   Suggest optimizing supply chain logistics or setting customer expectations with realistic delivery estimates.
6. **Encourage Decision-Making:**
   "Would you like us to run a small pilot program to measure the impact before making larger investments?"

BEHAVIORAL INTERVIEWS test not only technical skills but also communication, problem-solving, and decision-making abilities. By preparing with real-world scenarios and practicing clear, data-driven storytelling, candidates can significantly improve their chances of success in top tech interviews.

Chapter 10: Final Interview Prep & Mock Q&A

Section 1: Real-Time Mock Interview Scenarios

Preparing for a data analyst interview requires more than just technical knowledge. Recruiters often test your problem-solving ability, analytical thinking, and communication skills through real-time interview scenarios. Below are 15 real-world interview questions along with short but effective answers to help you navigate your final rounds with confidence.

1. Can you walk us through a data analysis project you worked on?

ANSWER:

Certainly. I worked on a sales data analysis project for an e-commerce company. The objective was to identify factors influencing customer retention. I gathered transactional data, cleaned it using SQL and Python, and conducted exploratory data analysis in Python's Pandas. Using statistical analysis, I found that personalized email marketing had a 20% higher retention rate. I visualized insights using Tableau, and my recommendations led to a refined marketing strategy, improving customer retention by 12%.

2. How do you handle missing or inconsistent data?

ANSWER:

I first assess the extent of missing values using descriptive statistics. If the missing data is minimal, I use imputation techniques like mean, median, or mode replacement. For categorical data, I use the most frequent category or predictive modeling. If a significant portion is missing, I analyze patterns and consider removing the variable if it's unreliable.

3. Explain the difference between supervised and unsupervised learning in data analysis.

ANSWER:

Supervised learning involves labeled data, where the outcome variable is known, such as regression or classification problems. In contrast, unsupervised learning works with unlabeled data, finding hidden patterns using clustering techniques like K-Means or PCA. Data analysts often use supervised learning for predictive modeling and unsupervised learning for customer segmentation.

4. How would you analyze website traffic data for a marketing campaign?

ANSWER:

I would start by gathering data from web analytics tools like Google Analytics. I'd segment the data based on traffic sources, user behavior, and engagement metrics. Using A/B testing, I would compare different campaign strategies. I'd also apply statistical tests to measure the effectiveness of campaign changes and visualize the results using dashboards.

5. How do you ensure data quality in your analysis?

ANSWER:

I use validation checks such as duplicate detection, missing value handling, and data type consistency. I perform cross-checks between different data sources, use summary statistics to spot anomalies, and apply business rules for validation. If necessary, I consult with domain experts to ensure accuracy.

6. What is the purpose of A/B testing in data analysis?

ANSWER:

A/B testing helps compare two versions of a webpage, product, or strategy to determine which performs better. It involves randomly splitting users into two groups, applying changes to one group, and measuring the impact on key performance indicators (KPIs) using statistical methods like t-tests.

7. How do you handle large datasets in analysis?

ANSWER:

For large datasets, I optimize data processing using indexing in SQL, apply efficient data structures in Python (Pandas, Dask), and leverage cloud computing solutions like Google BigQuery or AWS Redshift. I also use sampling techniques if full-scale computation isn't feasible.

8. What is the importance of data visualization in analysis?

ANSWER:

Data visualization helps communicate insights effectively. It enables stakeholders to grasp trends, correlations, and outliers quickly. I use visualization tools like Tableau, Power BI, and Matplotlib to create interactive reports that enhance decision-making.

9. How do you decide which statistical methods to apply in an analysis?

ANSWER:

The choice depends on the data type and objective. If analyzing relationships between variables, I use regression. For comparisons, I apply t-tests or ANOVA. When assessing distributions, I use chi-square tests. I ensure that assumptions of each method, such as normality or independence, are met before applying them.

10. What is SQL window function, and when would you use it?

ANSWER:

SQL window functions perform calculations across a set of table rows related to the current row without collapsing them into a single output. I use them for ranking, running totals, and moving averages, especially when analyzing sequential data like sales trends.

11. How do you detect and handle outliers in a dataset?

ANSWER:

I use statistical methods like the interquartile range (IQR) and Z-score. If an outlier results from an error, I correct or remove it. If it provides meaningful insights, I analyze its impact separately.

12. How would you measure the success of a business KPI?

ANSWER:

I compare KPI trends over time, benchmark against industry standards, and evaluate statistical significance in changes. Additionally, I use correlation analysis to link KPIs with business outcomes.

13. What is the difference between a database and a data warehouse?

ANSWER:

A database stores transactional data for day-to-day operations, while a data warehouse integrates and stores historical data for analysis. Databases support CRUD operations, whereas data warehouses support complex queries and reporting.

14. How would you communicate a complex data analysis result to a non-technical stakeholder?

ANSWER:

I focus on storytelling with clear visuals. I avoid technical jargon and use analogies. Presenting actionable insights and business impact in a simple way ensures stakeholder engagement.

15. What challenges have you faced in data analysis projects, and how did you overcome them?

ANSWER:

One challenge was dealing with inconsistent data formats from multiple sources. I overcame this by automating data cleaning processes using Python scripts and standardizing data collection templates.

Section 2: Handling Unexpected Questions with Confidence

IN AN INTERVIEW, YOU may face unexpected questions that assess your problem-solving ability, adaptability, and thought process. Here are 15 questions with structured responses.

16. What would you do if you encountered a dataset with no apparent patterns?

ANSWER:

I would explore different visualization techniques, apply transformations, and conduct advanced statistical tests. If no patterns emerge, I would question the dataset's relevance to the problem.

17. How do you handle disagreements with team members over data interpretations?

ANSWER:

I rely on data-driven evidence, conduct further validation, and involve a third-party perspective if needed. Open discussion and mutual understanding are key.

18. What steps do you take when a stakeholder requests urgent analysis?

ANSWER:

I clarify requirements, prioritize key metrics, use efficient data extraction techniques, and deliver an MVP (minimum viable product) analysis before refining details.

19. If given a dataset without context, how would you approach analysis?

ANSWER:

I start with exploratory data analysis (EDA), identify missing values, look for distribution trends, and research industry norms to infer context.

20. How do you balance speed and accuracy in data analysis?

ANSWER:

I prioritize accuracy by validating data sources, but I use automation and pre-built templates to speed up repetitive tasks without compromising quality.

21. What would you do if a dataset showed conflicting trends?

ANSWER:

I would verify data sources, check for seasonal variations, and conduct deeper segmentation to uncover root causes.

22. How do you decide which machine learning model to use for a problem?

ANSWER:

I evaluate factors like data size, interpretability, and business objectives. Simpler models like logistic regression work well for explainability, while complex models like XGBoost may be better for accuracy.

23. If a stakeholder asks for an unrealistic analysis, how do you handle it?

ANSWER:

I communicate constraints transparently and offer alternative solutions that provide actionable insights within feasibility limits.

24. What is the biggest misconception people have about data analysis?

ANSWER:

Many think data analysis is just about creating reports, but it's more about deriving meaningful insights that drive business decisions.

Section 3: Last-Minute Revision Strategies

PREPARING FOR A DATA analyst interview requires a combination of technical expertise, analytical thinking, and business acumen. In this section, we will discuss last-minute revision strategies to ensure you are well-prepared and confident before your final interview.

1. Review Key Concepts and Formulas

BEFORE YOUR INTERVIEW, revise core data analysis concepts, including:

- **Descriptive statistics**: Mean, median, mode, standard deviation, variance
- **Probability and distributions**: Normal distribution, binomial distribution, central limit theorem
- **SQL functions**: Aggregations, joins, window functions, CTEs
- **Data visualization best practices**: Choosing the right chart type, avoiding misleading visuals
- **A/B testing fundamentals**: Hypothesis testing, confidence intervals, p-values

2. Brush Up on SQL and Python/Pandas

SQL IS ESSENTIAL FOR data analysts. Make sure you are comfortable writing queries involving:

- Joins (INNER, LEFT, RIGHT, FULL)
- Window functions (RANK, DENSE_RANK, LEAD, LAG)
- Common Table Expressions (CTEs)
- Aggregate functions (SUM, COUNT, AVG, GROUP BY)
- Handling NULL values

For Python, review:

- Pandas: DataFrames, groupby(), pivot_table(), handling missing values
- NumPy: Arrays, statistical functions
- Matplotlib/Seaborn: Basic plotting, histograms, scatter plots

3. Solve Mock Case Studies

MANY INTERVIEWS INCLUDE case studies. Practice structuring your response using the **STAR (Situation, Task, Action, Result) framework**. Examples:

- How would you analyze a sudden drop in website traffic?
- How do you determine the success of a marketing campaign?
- What metrics would you track for a new product launch?

4. Practice Behavioral Questions

BEHAVIORAL QUESTIONS assess soft skills like problem-solving and teamwork. Be ready to answer:

- Tell me about a time you handled a challenging data project.
- Describe a time you found an error in a dataset. What did you do?
- Have you ever worked with a difficult stakeholder? How did you manage the situation?

5. Time Management & Mock Interviews

- Allocate at least **one hour per day** for focused preparation.
- Use **mock interviews** with a peer or an online platform to simulate real interview conditions.
- Keep responses **concise yet detailed**, ensuring clarity in explanations.

Section 4: Case Study – Cracking a FAANG Data Analyst Interview

FAANG (FACEBOOK, AMAZON, Apple, Netflix, Google) interviews are known for their rigor. Below, we will go through **real-time interview questions** that have been asked in FAANG data analyst interviews, along with **short expert answers.**

1. SQL Questions

Q1. WRITE A QUERY TO find the second highest salary from an Employee table.

A:

SELECT DISTINCT salary FROM Employee ORDER BY salary DESC LIMIT 1 OFFSET 1;

Q2. How do you handle NULL values in SQL?

A: Use COALESCE() or IFNULL() to replace NULLs with a default value.

Q3. Explain the difference between INNER JOIN and LEFT JOIN.

A:

- INNER JOIN returns only matching records.

- LEFT JOIN returns all records from the left table and matching ones from the right, filling unmatched rows with NULLs.

Q4. What is a Common Table Expression (CTE) and when would you use it?

A: A CTE is a temporary result set used within a query to improve readability and performance.

Q5. How would you optimize a slow SQL query?

A:

- Use **indexes** on frequently filtered columns.
- Avoid **SELECT ***; only retrieve necessary columns.
- Use **EXPLAIN** to analyze query execution plans.

- Optimize **joins** by ensuring indexed columns match data types.

---

2. Statistics & Probability

Q6. WHAT IS THE CENTRAL Limit Theorem?

A: It states that the sampling distribution of the mean approaches normality as sample size increases, regardless of population distribution.

Q7. Explain p-value in hypothesis testing.

A: The p-value measures the probability of obtaining the observed result under the null hypothesis. A low p-value (typically <0.05) suggests rejecting the null hypothesis.

Q8. What is A/B testing, and how do you determine if results are statistically significant?

A: A/B testing compares two versions of a webpage or product feature. Statistical significance is determined using metrics like **p-value, confidence intervals, and sample size calculations.**

Q9. When should you use a t-test vs. a z-test?

A: Use a **t-test** for small samples (n < 30) or unknown population variance; use a **z-test** for larger samples and known population variance.

Q10. How do you interpret a confidence interval?

A: A 95% confidence interval means that if the experiment were repeated multiple times, 95% of the time, the interval would contain the true parameter.

---

3. Python & Data Analysis

Q11. HOW DO YOU HANDLE missing values in Pandas?

A: Use dropna() to remove or fillna() to replace missing values.

Q12. What is the difference between loc and iloc in Pandas?

A:

- loc[] selects by **label**
- iloc[] selects by **position**

Q13. How would you detect outliers in a dataset?

A: Use methods like **IQR (Interquartile Range), Z-score,** or **box plots.**

Q14. Explain the difference between a histogram and a bar chart.

A: A **histogram** represents the distribution of numerical data, while a **bar chart** compares categorical data.

Q15. How would you calculate correlation between two variables in Python?

A: Use the Pandas method:

df['col1'].corr(df['col2'])

---

4. Business & Product Analytics

Q16. WHAT KPIS WOULD you track for an e-commerce business?

A: Conversion rate, average order value, customer retention rate, cart abandonment rate.

Q17. How do you measure the success of a product launch?

A: Track adoption rate, active users, revenue impact, and customer feedback.

Q18. How would you approach analyzing customer churn?

A: Identify patterns using **cohort analysis**, **survival analysis**, and **retention curves.**

Q19. What factors influence customer lifetime value (CLV)?

A: Purchase frequency, average order value, retention rate, and acquisition costs.

Q20. How would you improve a company's data-driven decision-making process?

A: By promoting **data literacy**, implementing **self-serve analytics**, and improving **data quality**.

---

5. Behavioral Questions

Q21. TELL ME ABOUT a time you worked on a challenging dataset.

A: Use STAR method: Situation, Task, Action, Result.

Q22. Have you ever made a mistake in your analysis? How did you fix it?

A: Acknowledge, correct, and implement a **quality control** process.

Q23. Describe a time when you had to present complex findings to a non-technical audience.

A: Use **simple language, visual aids, and analogies.**

Q24. How do you handle conflicting stakeholder requirements?

A: Prioritize based on **business impact and feasibility.**

Q25. What motivates you to be a data analyst?

A: Explain passion for **problem-solving, insights, and impact.**

This chapter covers essential last-minute strategies and real-time FAANG interview questions. With the right preparation and practice, you can confidently approach your data analyst interview.

www.ingramcontent.com/pod-product-compliance
Lightning Source LLC
LaVergne TN
LVHW022056200926
848481LV00003B/937